PETER GILL'S FIRST WORLD WAR QUIZ BOOK

Peter Gill

ISBN: 9798567234396

DEDICATION

To all that were there, of all sides.

Lest We Forget

CONTENTS

INTRODUCTION

The First World War, or The Great War as it is often referred to, was undoubtedly the defining historical event of the twentieth century. To many the images most easily identified with the war will be the mud and trenches of the Western Front in Flanders and Northern France where millions fought and died. But the war was far from a localised conflict, it was truly global and drew in men from all corners of the world. Ultimately it would change the world for ever. The destruction of life and landscape is familiar to all, but beyond that there were developments that we continue to live with today. Countries were lost and formed, dynasties were overthrown, rapid advances in technology and medicine were made, and indubitably the cause of votes for women and all men in Great Britain was enhanced.

This quiz book is intended as an informative and fun reflection of the Great War and a tribute to those, of all sides who served. There are questions for the novice war historian and for the expert. There are questions to encourage further reading and investigation and others to ease a tiring mind. There are rounds on the main protagonists, the more important battles, the war in the air and at sea, the weapons, the celebrities that played a part, and a host on general knowledge. There are also anagrams to decipher and films, books, quotes, poems and music to recognise.

I hope that you enjoy testing yourself with these questions, of which there are over 1000, and I hope it encourages you to further your interest and knowledge, no matter what level it already is.

Above all I hope and trust that this book, light-hearted as it is in many ways, creates some reflection for all of those that were there at the time.

Lest We Forget

Peter Gill – November 2020

THE QUESTIONS

QUIZ 1 - NICE AND EASY DOES IT

Some easy questions to get the ball rolling ……

1. What countries constituted the Triple Entente?

2. On what date did Britain go to war with Germany?

3. What was the term commonly used for the area of land between the frontline trenches of either army?

4. What countries constituted the Triple Alliance?

5. Ubiquitous during the war, soldiers would spend hours burning them out of the seams of their uniforms with candles, what were they?

6. As what was Manfred von Richthofen better known?

7. What were Very lights?

8. What is the common term for a concrete-reinforced machine gun position?

9. Awarded for valour 'in the presence of the enemy' what is the highest award given to members of the British Armed Forces?

10. What was the time and date that the guns finally fell silent on the Western Front signaling the end of the First World War?

QUIZ 2 – THE WINDS OF WAR

Ten questions on the events that led up to the war:

1. In what year did Great Britain and Belgium sign the Treaty of London, assuring Belgium's independence and neutrality?

2. Which annexed region of France by Germany following the Prussian War created an incendiary tension between the two countries?

3. Who said in 1898: There has been a constant tendency on the part of almost every nation to increase its armed force?

4. In what year was the Triple Entente of Great Britain, France and Russia formed?

5. Which crisis of 1911 led to secret discussions between France and Britain in which it was agreed that a British Expeditionary Force of 100,000 men would be landed in France within two weeks of any war breaking out with Germany?

6. Which notable French pacifist politician was murdered on July 31 1914 which helped to destabilise the French government and brought the inevitable war a step closer?

7. Where did the assassination of Archduke Ferdinand take place?

8. At the beginning of the war what was Bosnia-Herzegovina part of?

9. Who supposedly sent in a telegram to Kaiser Wilhelm II: *I foresee that very soon I shall be overwhelmed by the pressure forced upon me and be forced to take extreme measures which will lead to war. To try and avoid such a calamity as a European war I beg you in the name of our old friendship to do what you can to stop your allies from going too far. Nicky.*?

10. Who wrote in a personal letter, just one week before Britain was at war: *We are within measurable, or imaginable, distance of a real Armageddon. Happily there seems to be no reason why we should be anything more than spectators.*?

QUIZ 3 - IT STARTS

A selection of questions on the first days of the Great War:

1. What was the name of the Archduke Ferdinand's assassin?

2. With which terrorist organisation was the assassin associated?

3. Which country declared war on Serbia signalling what would become the commencement of the First World War?

4. What was the date of that declaration of war?

5. What small conflict on the French border on August 2 1914 is considered to be the first military action on the Western Front?

6. In Germany's invasion of Belgium, which strategic fortressed town saw the heaviest fighting between the defending army and the insurgents?

7. Approximately what was the total strength of the British Army on August 1 1914?

8. Who was Britain's foreign secretary who proved ineffective in warning Germany against threatening the neutrality of Belgium?

9. In which town in Belgium did Britain begin and end the war?

10. Who was in command of the British Expeditionary Force at the commencement of the war?

QUIZ 4 - GENERAL KNOWLEDGE

Test your general knowledge of the First World War with this mix of questions:

1. What was the name of Archduke Ferdinand's wife who was killed alongside him?

2. Who did the British press often refer to as Little Willie and Big Willie?

3. What is the name of the sculpture unveiled in the Australian Memorial Park at Fromelles in 1998 which shows Australian Sergeant Simon Fraser carrying a wounded soldier on his shoulder?

4. At the beginning of the war what was the minimum height requirement for men to enlist?

5. Who were the two cinematographers who shot the documentary film *The Battle of the Somme* in 1916?

6. The Western Front trench system stretched for approximately 400 miles from the Belgian Coast at Nieuwpoort in the north to France's frontier with which country in the south?

7. On August 22 1914 what did cavalryman Edward Thomas of the 4th Royal Irish Dragoon Guards do at Casteau?

8. What was the name of the British volunteer nurse, mother of politician Shirley Williams, who wrote the best-selling memoirs *Testament of Youth* about her wartime experiences?

9. What were the nicknames given to the three medals ensemble consisting of 1914-15 Star, the British War Medal and the Victory Medal?

10. From what language is the term 'khaki' taken?

QUIZ 5 - MILITARY BREAKDOWN

A bit of a generalisation and approximation, but what assemblage did the following military personnel command and how many men were in them?

1. A Private

2. Corporal or Lance Corporal

3. Lieutenant or Second-Lieutenant

4. Captain

5. Lieutenant-Colonel

6. Brigadier-General

7. Major-General

8. Lieutenant-General

9. General

10. Field-Marshall

QUIZ 6 - INITIALLY SPEAKING

The following initials would have been familiar abbreviations during the Great War. What are they short for?

1. B.E.F.

2. R.F.C.

3. D.C.M.

4. V.A.D.

5. P.P.C.L.I.

6. D.S.O.

7. A.I.F.

8. C.C.S.

9. S.M.L.E.

10. W.A.A.C.

QUIZ 7 - RANK AND FILE

The following questions all refer to officer ranks during the First World War

1. What was the highest rank in the British navy?

2. What encouraging rank in the French Army is one below a Sous-Lieutenant?

3. If you were an Oberstleutnant in the German Army, what would the corresponding rank in the British Army be?

4. In which army were the higher ranks of Birinci Ferik, Ferik and Mirliva?

5. How many 'stars' would a Lieutenant General wear in the United States of America Army?

6. A Potpukovnik in the Serbian Army would be ranked as what in the French Army?

7. What is the missing Italian rank: Colonello, Tenente Colonello, Maggioro, ?, Tenente

8. Rank in descending seniority from left to right these British Army officers: Captain, Major-General, Colonel, Brigadier-General, Major, Lieutenant-Colonel

9. What was the Portuguese equivalent rank to the French and British Colonel?

10. What was the highest rank in the German Army?

QUIZ 8 - NAME THE COUNTRY

In which present day countries did the following battles and offensives take place?

1. Battle of Scimitar Hill

2. Battle of the Piave River

3. Battle of the Vistula River

4. Battle of Bazargic (also known as Battle of Dobrich)

5. Morava Offensive

6. Battle of Rufiji Delta

7. Battle of Florina

8. Battle of Magdhaba

9. Battle of Qurna

10. Battle of Hulluch

QUIZ 9 - TOMMIES' SLANG

What do the following slang terms that were used by the British Tommies translate to?

1. Alley tootsweet

2. Army Rocks

3. Babbling Brook

4. Baby's Head

5. To go barpoo

6. Barrow Wallah

7. Bathmats

8. Battle Bowler

9. Bees and honey

10. Blighty

QUIZ 10 - WORLD LEADERS

At the beginning of the Great War who were the following world leaders?

1. The Prime Minister of Great Britain?

2. The President of the United States of America?

3. The Prime Minister of Bulgaria?

4. The Tzar of Russia?

5. The King of Italy?

6. The Sultan of the Ottoman Empire?

7. The King of Belgium?

8. The German Emperor?

9. The King of Spain?

10. The Emperor of Japan?

QUIZ 11 - ANAGRAMS

Decipher the following anagrams to reveal the name of a person associated with the Great War

1. Admirals Goldfish Haulage

2. Chalet Devil

3. Werewolf Din

4. Twinkies Revolted Cajun

5. Northern Bofin Havoc

6. Perilled Linens

7. Few Arabian

8. Offhanded Charms Arlin

9. Abilene Mini Followers

10. Kerrin Handcuffed Zandra

QUIZ 12 - GENERAL KNOWLEDGE 2

Another selection of general knowledge questions on the war:

1. In what Belgian town was the 'Everyman's Club' Talbot House (referred by the Tommies as TocH)?

2. At which corner would you find Canada's Brooding Soldier memorial to the victims of the gas attack of the Second Battle of Ypres?

3. Ypres was often referred to as being in a 'salient' and hence more dangerous than many other sectors of the war. What is a salient and therefore why was it so much more dangerous?

4. During the war the Principal Allies were Great Britain, France, Russia, Italy, USA and one other. What was the other country?

5. What fate did Lance Corporal Frederick Hawthorne, Chi Ming Hei, Corporal Frederick Ives, Private William Roberts and Private Arthur Wild all suffer?

6. Who was the editor of *The Wipers Times*?

7. On which part of the Turkish coast did allied troops land on April 25 1915?

8. What was the name of the German helmet famous for its spike?

9. The 1st Battalion of which British dominion's regiment suffered a 75% casualty rate within half an hour of its assault on the Germans at Beaumont Hamel on the opening day of the offensive?

10. Who is regarded as the oldest British serviceman to have died in the Great War?

QUIZ 13 - ARMY SIGNALLERS' CODE

For a private in the British Army of the Great War, what were the Army Signaller's code words for the following letters?

1. M

2. D

3. L

4. W

5. N

6. T

7. Q

8. S

9. A

10. J

QUIZ 14 - WHO AM I?

Identify these famous people from the descriptions:

1. A French pioneering aviator and fighter pilot, I was in a German POW camp for almost three years before escaping to return to active service. I was shot down and killed on October 5 1918. In 1928 a tennis stadium was named in my honour which now hosts the French Open Tennis Tournament.

2. I was commissioned into the Somerset Light Infantry as a Second Lieutenant whilst still studying at Oxford University, on my 19th birthday I arrived at the front line in the Somme Valley. On April 15 1918, I was wounded and two of my colleagues were killed by a British shell falling short of its target. After the war I became famous for my tales of Narnia.

3. A Belgian General responsible for the military education of King Albert I. I commanded the forts at Liege against the German Army but was eventually captured and saw out the war as a prisoner of war.

4. Born in South Africa, I served in the Canadian Army on the Western Front as a diminutive bugler and stretcher bearer when just sixteen years of age. After the war I stayed in England and found fame through my holiday camps.

5. I was commissioned into the Royal Warwickshire Regiment in February 1915 as a Second Lieutenant, the following year whilst serving in France on the Somme I was injured and invalided back to Britain. I then went on to write propaganda articles for Military Intelligence. After the war I became well-loved for my stories about my son Christopher Robin and his stuffed toys.

6. A barrister and a distinguished scholar, my father was Prime Minister when I was killed leading my men near Ginchy at the Battle of Flers-Courcelette.

7. A successful author after the war, especially known for the book Tarka The Otter, I went to France with the London Rifles in November 1914 and witnessed the Christmas Truce of that year. I would also later serve with the Machine Gun Corps, but spent much of the war recovering variously from trench foot, dysentery and the effects of gas.

8. A Lieutenant in the Lancashire Fusiliers, I saw action on the Somme participating in the capture of the Schwaben Redoubt and the Leipzig Salient. I was invalided out of action soon after having contracted trench fever and never saw action again. After the war I became an Oxford don and created the world of Middle Earth.

9. I joined up with the Artists' Rifles in November 1915 but in September of the following year I was given a commission with the East Surrey Regiment as a Second Lieutenant, being sent with them later that month to France. I was wounded in action on August 2 1917 during the Battle of Passchendaele and was invalided back to Britain. After the war my play *Journey's End,* based on my one wartime experiences, was a great success. I also wrote screenplays including *Goodbye Mr Chips* and *The Dam Busters.*

10. I was born in Italy of Polish-Belarussian descent, but I fought in the French infantry before acquiring a serious shrapnel wound to my temple. I was a famous poet, playwright, author and art-critic and have been credited with creating the term 'surrealism'. I died on November 9 1918, a victim of the Spanish flu pandemic.

QUIZ 15 - IT'S A DATE

Name the date!

1. Of the assassination of Archduke Ferdinand.

2. When Germany declared war on France.

3. The deadliest day in the history of the French army when 27,000 French soldiers were killed.

4. That Italy joined the Triple Entente and declared war on Austria-Hungary?

5. That an eight hour truce was called between the opposing armies in Gallipoli in order that the dead lying in No Man's Land could be buried.

6. That the ANZACS left Gallipoli.

7. That conscription in Great Britain came into force for the first time.

8. That Lochnagar Crater was formed just south of the village of La Boiselle?

9. That Portuguese soldiers first see action on the Western Front.

10. That Private George Edwin Ellison of the 5th Royal Irish Lancers killed.

QUIZ 16 - POLITICIANS AT WAR

Test your knowledge of the politicians who fought in the Great War:

1. A veteran of the Boer War and a Unionist politician, who was the first serving MP to lose his life during the war?

2. Four future British Prime Ministers saw action in the war, Winston Churchill, Clement Attlee and Harold Macmillan and which other?

3. Which Conservative MP from Chorley, was the only cabinet minister to serve in the ranks, volunteering for the R.A.M.C., he then became a harsh critic of the war, leadership and politicians, such as Churchill who used their contacts to obtain elevated positions in the military?

4. Which MP for Heywood in Lancashire lost his life in Gallipoli in September 1915?

5. Which trade unionist and MP for Stoke-on-Trent became a lieutenant-colonel of the 21st Middlesex regiment and served with them in France?

6. Which serving Irish Nationalist MP joined the Royal Munster Fusiliers serving with them as a captain at Loos, believing that it was his duty to serve and that in so doing would put power to his political aims?

7. Churchill uniquely began the war as a cabinet minister, then went to serve in the trenches and ended up back in political office. In which position did he oversee the disastrous Gallipoli campaign?

8. Which serving Liberal Unionist MP for Cardiff was shot and killed whilst rallying his troops against a German counter-attack at the Battle of Loos on October 2 1915?

9. A second cousin to a famous soldier-poet and a MP for Hythe, he spent much of the war working as a secretary, adviser and liaison officer to General Haig. Who was he?

10. Commissioned as a second lieutenant in the Middlesex Yeomanry in December 1914, he later became an officer in the RFC. He was awarded the DSO in 1917 and DFC in 1918. He served as both a Liberal and Labour MP, the latter for whom both his son and grandson served, who was he?

QUIZ 17 - NAME THE BATTLE

Identify the battle from the following descriptions:

1. A highly successful British campaign commencing June 7 1917 with the exploding of 19 mines.

2. Enacted between May 31 and June 1 1916 off the North Sea coast of Denmark.

3. The first big offensive launched mainly by American forces, fought between September 12-15 1918.

4. Held between September 6-12 1914 this was the battle which marked the first major German defeat.

5. Lasting for ten months, this was the longest battle of the war.

6. The first day was the worst in British military history with almost 60,000 casualties, of which almost 20,000 were killed.

7. Part of the Gallipoli campaign, this battle was the only success for the Allies over the Ottoman Empire, with the capture of their objective on August 8 1915.

8. The first use of tanks in combat occurring on September 15 1916.

9. The only German offensive of 1915 commencing on the night of April 22 with the first use of gas by the Germans on the Western Front.

10. Part of the Arab Revolt fought on July 6 1917 when Auda ibu Tayi's forces, being advised by T.E. Lawrence defeated the Ottoman Empire.

QUIZ 18 - THE CANADIANS

Some questions on the Canadians who came across the North Atlantic to serve alongside the British Forces:

1. From which port city did the majority of Canadian soldiers set sail to serve overseas?

2. Before being sent to the Western Front, where had the men of the Newfoundland Regiment been in action?

3. The gas attack of April 22 1915 was their first major action on the Ypres Salient, what did the Canadian troops do to cope with the gas that had caused such havoc in the French lines?

4. The Canadians were issued with larrigans in 1915. What were they?

5. The most decorated Canadian of the war, he won the VC, DSO and Bar, MC and two Bars, two Italian Silver Medals for Military Valour and the French Croix de Guerre. Who was this fighter ace?

6. What date is known as Memorial Day in Newfoundland and Labrador?

7. Which battle in 1917 saw all four divisions of the Canadian Corps fight together as one formation for the first time, and because of their victory is seen as a pivotal point in shaping Canada as a nation?

8. The Third Battle of Ypres, more commonly referred to as the Battle of Passchendaele ended with the capture of this small village by the Canadian Corps. What was the date that they liberated Passchendaele?

9. Which Canadian officer of the 5th Canadian Mounted Rifles, instrumental in the eventual victory at Passchendaele, won a VC during the action and also was awarded a Military Cross and Distinguished Service Order and promoted to Lieutenant Colonel during the war?

10. Lieutenant-General Arthur Currie considered it to be the Canadians' 'single greatest feat', in which battle did it occur?

QUIZ 19 - ALL AT SEA

A first selection of questions pertaining to the maritime war:

1. Impressively armed and with steam turbine propulsion, it quickly became hugely influential and often copied, what did the Royal Navy first launch in 1906?

2. Which British ship became the first of the Royal Navy's to be sunk when it struck a mine on August 6 1914 in the Thames Estuary causing the deaths of 132 crewmen?

3. On August 28 1914, under the command of Admiral David Beatty the Royal Navy defeated the German Navy in their first naval battle of the war. Occurring in the North Sea off the German coast, what was the battle named?

4. Who had to resign his post as First Sea Lord, Admiral of the British Fleet shortly after the war began?

5. Which German Vice Admiral was killed at the Battle of the Falkland Islands on December 8 1914?

6. The first Royal Australian Navy battle occurred on November 9 1914 off the Cocos Islands. Which German cruiser was sunk by HMAS Sydney during that battle?

7.What German weapon destroyed more British ships than anything else?

8. What ship was Lord Kitchener sailing on when it struck a German mine and sunk, killing him and many others on board on June 5 1916?

9. What raid made by the Royal Navy on April 23 1918 was an attempt to block a Belgian port by sinking obsolete ships in the canal entrance to stop German boats from leaving?

10. For a while on HMS Glasgow there was a passenger that had been saved from a sinking German ship but was later auctioned off to raise fund for the British Red Cross. What was the passenger's given name?

QUIZ 20 - ANAGRAMS 2

Decipher the following anagrams to reveal a place associated with the Great War:

1. Unhinged Berlin

2. Etty Royce Cement

3. Amenable Mouth

4. Abilene Commoner Prankster

5. IP Zeroes

6. Elf Morsel

7. Curve Rover Canon

8. Lilia Glop

9. Elvis Laser

10. Actor Poet

QUIZ 21 - MEDICAL ADVANCEMENTS

Answer these questions that highlight the medical advancements that were brought on by the Great War:

1. What was the name of the type of splint which was designed to immobilise the leg to stop further bleeding and align fractured pieces, introduced to the Western Front in 1916 which reduced the rate of mortality from fractures (particularly of the femur) from 80% to 20%?

2. Using his tubed pedicle technique for what type of surgery did New Zealander Harold Gillies become famous?

3. Caused by the bacteria *Clostridia* what often deadly infection was rampant amongst those wounded whilst in the mud and dirt of France and Flanders?

4. Serving in the Royal Army Medical Corps during the war where he studied the efficacy of antiseptics that were being used, which Scottish bacteriologist went on to discover penicillin after the war?

5. The Princess Louise Scottish Hospital in Erskine and the Queen Mary Convalescent Hospital in Roehampton were both opened solely for treating amputees. What did their experiences and investigations subsequently make great improvements to?

6. Which American surgeon, whilst working at the American Ambulance Hospital in France, also credited as being the first surgeon to have succeeded in a direct blood transfusion, introduced doctors to a method of anaesthesia using nitrous-oxide which would have a profound effect on survival rates?

7. Which influential American neurosurgeon, a pioneer of brain surgery, operated in France during 1917 and 1918 where he treated 133 soldiers with brain wounds, cutting the operative mortality rate in his time from 50% to 29%?

8. Noting the high mortality rate from infected wounds and the poor results from the antiseptics used, a technique was eventually adopted using a new solution of sodium hypochlorite and the thorough irrigation and cleansing of wounds. What was this technique called?

9. In 1914, which French scientist went to the front with the Union des Femmes de France and equipped several hundred vehicles with X-ray machines, effectively making a radiological ambulance service?

10. What did Canadian surgeon Bruce Robertson add to blood to allow it to be conserved and transported, consequently enabling doctors close to the front to carry out more rapid and therefore more effective transfusions?

QUIZ 22 - GENERAL KNOWLEDGE 3

Some more questions to test your general knowledge of the war!

1. What was the name of the humourist and cartoonist who created the popular character of 'Old Bill'?

2. Although he didn't see action he did join the British Expeditionary Force in France, in which battalion was the Prince of Wales (later Edward VIII) commissioned?

3. During the Easter Rising in Ireland of 1916, what building on O'Connell Street, Dublin was taken over by the rebels?

4. Which Music Hall star was nicknamed *Britain's best recruiting sergeant*?

5. Who did the Tommies refer to as Red Caps?

6. Although his age is now contested, who has long been regarded as the youngest British soldier to have been killed in the Great War?

7. Written by Canadian doctor John McCrae, which poem is credited with the adoption of the red poppy as a token of remembrance?

8. Of what type of stone are the majority of Commonwealth War Graves headstones?

9. What was the common brand of tinned ration consisting of sliced vegetables in a thin soup or gravy?

10. Why were tanks thus named?

QUIZ 23 - IT'S ALL ABOUT THE NUMBERS

All the answers are numbers ......

1. The time, day and month of the Armistice.

2. The number of British army chaplains that were killed during the war.

3. The number of men shot at dawn by the Australians.

4. The hill in Belgium where Benjamin Handley Geary, Geoffrey Harold Woolley, Edward Warner, Edward Dwyer and George Rowland Patrick Roupell all won their Victoria Crosses.

5. The number of mines that were detonated at the beginning of the Battle of Messines in June 1917.

6. The number of days of the Battle of the Somme.

7. To the nearest thousand, the number of names inscribed on the Tyne Cot Memorial to the Missing.

8. The number of British Generals killed during the war.

9. The age of the youngest, authenticated British soldier to serve during the war.

10. The number of Canadians who won Victoria Crosses during the war.

QUIZ 24 - THE WAR ON THE HOME FRONT

Ten questions on how the war came directly to Britain.

1. What was DORA?

2. On December 16 1914 the German Navy conducted a raid on which three British ports resulting in 592 casualties?

3. On the night of January 19 1915 which two British towns were attacked by German Zeppelins killing four civilians>

4. What were sometimes handed to ununiformed men to shame them into serving their country?

5. What tragedy occurred near Gretna Green on May 22 1915?

6. What was established in 1916 by Act of Parliament as principally a way to conserve coal in Great Britain?

7. Which British newspaper, reported the Somme battle on July 3 1916 as: *EVERYTHING HAS GONE WELL - Our troops have successfully carried out their missions, all counter-attacks have been repulsed and large numbers of prisoners taken.*

8. Why were children encouraged to collect 3,000 tons of conkers in 1917 for the war effort?

9. What tragedy occurred on July 1 1918 in Chilwell, Nottinghamshire?

10. In which year did the British Government bring in food rationing?

QUIZ 25 - ITALY

Some questions to test you about Italy's involvement in the Great War.

1. Who was the Italian Prime Minister who brought the country into the war on the side of the Triple Entente?

2. What was signed on April 26 1915 by Italy, France, Russia and Great Britain?

3. Who was the Italian commander-in-chief whose frontal assault tactics against the Austro-Hungarians along the Isonzo River cost the lives of hundreds of thousands of Italian soldiers?

4. Who was the first of the 650,000 Italian soldiers killed in the war?

5. Enrico Toti achieved immortality for his courage when serving as a sniper on the Italian Front, what was particularly remarkable about him?

6. What is the nickname given to the fighting in the Alpine sector of the Italian Front chiefly between Italy and Austria-Hungary?

7. At which battle, commencing October 24 1918 were the Italians victorious over Austria-Hungary?

8. On which date did Austria-Hungary and Italy sign an armistice?

9. From 1916 the Italian 35th Division fought on the Salonika Front as part of which multi-national force?

10. By what was the Italian navy known during the Great War?

QUIZ 26 - IT'S AN ANIMAL THING

Which animals would you associate with the following basic clues?

1. Newfoundland Park, Beaumont Hamel.

2. Captain Jack Seeley, Warrior.

3. Australian 10th Battalion.

4. Famously reported as growing to the size of cats, the scourge of both sides in the trenches.

5. HMS Dreadnought, Togo.

6. Cher Ami.

7. John Simpson Kirkpatrick, Gallipoli.

8. Harry Colebourn, Winnipeg.

9. Thomas Ward, Lizzie.

10. South African Infantry, Jackie.

QUIZ 27 - GALLIPOLI

What are the answers to these questions on the campaign in the Dardanelles?

1. Which British admiral was initially in charge of spearheading the operation at Gallipoli?

2. What was the first ship to be sunk in the campaign?

3. The British landed on the peninsula on five beaches, of which three bore catastrophic casualty rates. What were the beaches named?

4. Which strategic hill changed hands five times between May 2-3 1915 as 4000 Turkish troops held off an ANZAC force 3 times their size, largely because the attackers were poorly organised, reinforcements were delayed and commanders were not informed in time?

5. Who resigned as First Sea Lord in May 1915 from frustration of the mishandling of the Gallipoli invasion by the then First Lord of the Admiralty Winston Churchill?

6. As the weather got warmer in the Dardanelles, disease amongst the soldiers in the trenches began to spread. What was the most common disease that affected them?

7. Which inspirational frontline commander of the Ottoman troops would go on to become the first President of the Republic of Turkey?

8. On May 25 1915 the HMS Triumph sank. What caused this disaster which also resulted in the loss of 70 soldiers?

9. Which British lieutenant-general commanded the Anzacs for most of the Gallipoli campaign?

10. Why is the grave of the extraordinary British officer, Lieutenant-Colonel Charles Doughty-Wylie, killed on April 26 1915 and posthumously awarded a VC, unique on the Gallipoli Peninsula?

QUIZ 28 - IT'S ALL UP IN THE AIR

A selection of questions on the war in the air!

1. Why did countries begin marking their aircraft under the wings?

2. Why were Zeppelin's thus named?

3. With 72 confirmed victories, who was the Royal Air Force's most successful pilot?

4. Which single-seat German fighter plane was the first to use a synchronized machine gun?

5. Which country marked their aircraft with a green centre circle followed by a white middle circle and a red outer circle?

6. A top British flying ace he was awarded a VC posthumously for leading an attack on a squadron of German fighter planes commanded by Lother von Richthofen. Who was he?

7. What type of aircraft was the Handley Page 0/400?

8. When was the Royal Air Force formed?

9. Not brought into action until April 1918, which was the first Sopwith aeroplane to have an armoured fuselage?

10. Which German became, on August 20 1918, the first night fighter ace?

QUIZ 29 - STARS IN THE WARS

Name the following stars of stage and screen that saw action in the Great War from the following clues:

1. As a second lieutenant in the Scottish Liverpool Regiment he won a Military Cross and found fame on screen, particularly being associated with his role as Sherlock Holmes.

2. Serving as a lance corporal in the Somerset Light Infantry he was wounded in the German lines at Guedecourt in 1916. After the war he became a playwright and actor, best known for his role as Private Charles Godfrey in Dad's Army.

3. Serving in the French infantry he was wounded and captured by the Germans, being imprisoned for two years at Altengrabow POW camp. After the war he became a cabaret and Hollywood film star, notably in 1958's *Gigi.*

4. This British actor was an OSCAR winner for his role in the 1947 film *A Double Life.* He was amongst the first territorial troops to see action in Flanders but was blown into the air by a shell at Messines in October 1914.

5. A renowned German film director of films such as *Metropolis* (1926), *M* (1931) and *Fury* (1936), he served in the Imperial Landwehr Field Gun Division being wounded twice in eight days on the Russian Front in 1916.

6. Serving in the Royal Hungarian Infantry with distinction, he is an icon of the screen horror genre, perhaps most famously as Dracula in 1931.

7. Serving in the London Scottish Regiment he was severely gassed at Vimy Ridge in November 1916 resulting in the loss of 90% of the sight in his right eye. He became a frequent screen villain and co-starred in *Casablanca.*

8. Hit 11 times in his leg at the Battle of Cambrai in 1917, he would become the archetypal screen Dr Watson of the interwar period.

9. This future American Hollywood actor in films such as *Gung Ho!, Ride Lonesome* and *Frontier Marshal* served with the 2nd Trench Mortar Battalion of the 19th Field Artillery in the spring of 1918.

10. This iconic Hollywood star served in the US Navy on the USS Leviathan, predominantly ferrying US soldiers and German POWs to and from Europe. Films such as *The African Queen, The Maltese Falcon* and *Casablanca* have given him legendary screen status.

QUIZ 30 - WHAT'S THE REAL NAME?

What were the proper names of the towns and villages that the Tommies referred to as the following:

1. Wipers
2. Mucky Farm
3. Bert
4. Sally Booze
5. Baloo
6. Pop
7. White Sheet
8. About Turn
9. Plugstreet Wood
10. Devil's Wood

QUIZ 31 - NAME THE POEM AND ITS AUTHOR

From which poems by soldier poets of the Great War are these the first lines and who wrote them?

1. If I should die, think only this of me:

2. "Jack fell as he'd have wished", the Mother said

3. Kiss the maid and pass her round

4. You are blind like us. Your hurt no man designed,

5. Bent double, like old beggars under sacks,

6. We found the little captain at the head;

7. Nudes - stark and glistening,

8. Who died on the wires, and hung there, one of two

9. Rain, midnight rain, nothing but the wild rain

10. Morning, if this late withered light can claim

QUIZ 32 - ANAGRAMS 3

Decipher the following anagrams to reveal a weapon associated with the Great War:

1. Asgard Smut

2. Chicks Maneuvering

3. Guam Minx

4. Plene Zip

5. Took Armrests

6. Bea Bright

7. IBM Lobs ML

8. Mermen Waffler

9. Eileen Fled

10. Thug Adorned

QUIZ 33 - GENERAL KNOWLEDGE 4

More questions to test your general knowledge of the Great War!

1. What name was given to the British battalions of men between 4 feet 10 inches and 5 feet 3 inches tall who were previously ineligible due to their stature?

2. What was the nickname adopted by American soldiers?

3. The Imperial War Cabinet met three times and consisted of representatives from seven nations – Canada, Australia, New Zealand, South Africa and the United Kingdom were five, which were the other two?

4. In October 1914 the Belgian Army thwarted the German advance and saved the port of Nieuport, what creative tactic forced the Germans back?

5. Who were referred to as K1 (K One)?

6. What was the family name of the Russian Imperial family at the time of the war?

7. Which disastrous battle for the Allies of 1915 saw the first use by the British of gas as a weapon?

8. Which war poet wrote the volume of poems entitled *Songs of the Field*?

9. What is the Turkish word for Gallipoli?

10. The founding members of the 170 (Tunnelling) Company, Royal Engineers were dubbed the Manchester Moles, which engineer, officer and politician was their founder?

QUIZ 34 - NAME THE VICTORIA CROSS WINNER

Identify the Victoria Cross awardees from the following descriptions:

1. The first British pilot to shoot down a German airship over Britain and the first person to be awarded the Victoria Cross for action in the United Kingdom.

2. Posthumously awarded the Victoria Cross for his actions on July 1 1916 when he threw himself on a box of live grenades to save the lives of his comrades.

3. Serving with the 89th Punjabis at Mesopotamia in April 1916 he held off the enemy with, firstly, his machine gun for three attacks, then with rifle fire. On withdrawal he aided a badly wounded man but then returned to his post to collect arms and ammunition.

4. A double VC winner. Having won his first medal in the 2nd Boer War, he was awarded his second for action in October and November 1914 when he rescued a great number of wounded men, whilst under fire near Zonnebeke in Belgium.

5. Which Indian Muslim jamadar (later promoted to subedar) was presented with his Victoria Cross at the Royal Pavilion Military Hospital in Brighton by King George V, for his courage on April 26 1915 during the Second Battle of Ypres.

6. Commander of the HMS Prize, he was given his VC for his efforts near the Scilly Isles when, though his ship was badly damaged by a U-boat he remained with a skeleton crew to see off the vessel.

7. On 16 November 1915 he spotted a badly-wounded soldier lying in no man's land, so, aided by a Medical Corporal, he tried to rescue him. After one failed attempt, they got to the wounded man and lifted him but the Medical Corporal was shot. He then bandaged up the Corporal and carried him back to the British lines, returning to bring the first wounded soldier to safety.

8. Observing men being held down by machine gun fire on the first day of the Battle of Passchendaele he ran 300 yards under fire to capture a machine gun and its crew, then continued and brought in 12 further prisoners.

9. Serving with the RFC on June 2 1917 he completed a solo mission that saw him shoot down three enemy aircraft and destroy more on the ground, for which he was duly awarded the VC.

10. On 3 October 1918 he earned a Victoria Cross for his 'bravery, initiative and devotion to duty'. Having heard that wounded men had been left behind during a retreat at Mannequin Hill, he went alone in the face of fierce enemy fire, and on three separate occasions carried casualties on his back to safety then tended to them for the next 48 hours.

QUIZ 35 - RUSSIA

Some questions on Russia's involvement in the War To End All Wars:

1. On what date did Russia enter the war?

2. Who was Russia's influential foreign minister at the commencement of the war and until July 1916?

3. Which Russian general committed suicide after the Russian Second Army's almost total destruction by Germany at the Battle of Tannenberg?

4. On September 7 1914 Russian pilot Pyotr Nesterov made aerial warfare history. What was he the first to accomplish?

5. The Black Sea Raid against Russian ports on October 29 1914 was the arrival of which power into the war?

6. In January 1915 Russian troops at Bolimov were attacked by German shells loaded with gas resulting in more than 1000 deaths. What type of gas was it?

7. Known as the 'June Advance' or more often after the brilliant Russian general and military tactician in charge, what was the great victory for the Russian Army against the Central Powers between June and September 1916?

8. What was the name of the Russian general that lost the Battle of the Masurian Lakes?

9. Who ordered the Russian offensive of July 1 1917?

10. After the Bolshevik Revolution what was Lenin's first decree?

QUIZ 36 - NAME THAT TUNE

From which songs, popular in the First World War, did the following lyrics come?

1. She'd do it for wine, she'd do it for rum, and sometimes even for chewing gum.

2. Goodbye Piccadilly, goodbye Leicester Square.

3. If you've a lucifer to light your fag, smile boy that's the style.

4. No more church parades on Sunday, no more putting in for leave.

5. They were summoned from the hillside, they were called in from the glen.

6. A garden of Eden just made for two, with nothing to mar our joy.

7. You were with the wenches, while we were in the trenches, facing the German foe.

8. Though it's hard to part I know, I'll be tickled to death to go!

9. She is watching by the poplars, Colinette with the sea-blue eyes.

10. Johnnie get your gun, get your gun, get your gun.

QUIZ 37 - THE HISTORIANS

Who were the authors of the following influential histories of the Great War:

1. The First Day On The Somme (1971)

2. The Donkeys (1961)

3. Goodbye To All That: An Autobiography (1929)

4. With A Machine Gun To Cambrai (1968)

5. *Kitchener's Army : The Raising of the New Armies, 1914-16 (1988)*

6. They Called It Passchendaele (1990)

7. History of the First World War (1930)

8. Storm of Steel (1920)

9. Seven Pillars of Wisdom (1926)

10. The Price of Glory: Verdun 1916 (1962)

QUIZ 38 - WHERE AM I BURIED?

Where are the following buried or commemorated?

1. Private John Parr (the first British casualty on the Western Front)

2. Valentine Joe Strudwick (15 year old casualty from Dorking)

3. Gilbert Talbot (brother of Neville and who 'Talbot House' was named after)

4. John Kipling (son of Rudyard Kipling)

5. Wilfred Owen (poet)

6. George Butterworth (composer of the *A Shropshire Lad Rhapsody*)

7. Noel Godfrey Chavasse (double VC winner)

8. Rupert Brooke (poet)

9. Edith Cavell (nurse)

10. Lord Kitchener (Right Honourable Horatio Herbert Kitchener of Khartoum)

QUIZ 39 - CAPITAL CITIES

A little bit of historical geography! At the start of the Great War what were the capital cities of the following:

1. Norway

2. Austria-Hungary

3. Bavaria

4. Saxony

5. Wurttemburg

6. Russian Empire

7. Albania

8. Ottoman Empire

9. Brazil

10. Newfoundland

QUIZ 40 - INSPECTING THE MORSE

Developed in 1837 by Samuel Morse, his eponymous code was in great use during the war. What letters do the following denote?

1. - - (dash dash)

2. - - - (dash dash dash)

3. . - . (dot, dash, dot)

4. . . . (dot, dot, dot)

5. . (dot)

6. - . - . (dash, dot, dash, dot)

7. - . . (dash, dot, dot)

8. . - - (dot, dash, dash)

9. . - - - - (dot, dash, dash, dash, dash)

10. . . . . – (dot, dot, dot, dot, dash)

QUIZ 41 - I SPY

A selection of questions on espionage in the war:

1. Who was the first German spy to be executed in Great Britain during the war?

2. How many spies were executed in total in Britain, the last being Ludovico Zender on April 11 1916?

3. What was unique about Robert Rosenthal's execution of the twelve?

4. Which popular novelist and playwright served with the Red Cross and in the ambulance corps during the war before being recruited into the Secret Intelligence Service in 1916?

5. By what name was Margaretha Zelle the woman executed as a German spy better known as?

6. Which British nurse was executed as a spy by the Germans on October 12 1915?

7. Which popular British author of children's books was given the code name S.76 and gave information to the British Secret Intelligence Service about his travels and contacts in Russia during the war?

8. The Germans had a spy school in Antwerp called the Kriegsnachrichtenstelle which was headed by which impressive woman, nicknamed Fräulein Doktor?

9. Who was the Belgian woman who volunteered for the Belgian Red Cross but was later hired by British Intelligence, working for them until her capture by the Germans in February 1916, being executed on April 1?

10. Commanded by General Charles-Joseph Dupont what was the name of the French intelligence agency that was operating throughout the war?

QUIZ 42 - ANAGRAMS 4

Some more anagrams! This time decipher the following to reveal a term associated with the Great War:

1. Landlines Differs

2. Fibrinogen Gallivanter

3. Acrostic Visor

4. Krupp Ably Courteous

5. Piffle Channels

6. Antimony Thereafter Whiniest

7. Reinformed Ameliorates Lemme

8. Adkins Quipper Flawed

9. Solemn Fangos

10. Ardyce Exhibitioner Profits

QUIZ 43 - GENERAL KNOWLEDGE 5

Yet more general knowledge questions to get your brain working:

1. What weapon, often used in gas attacks by the British, was mortar-like and could hurl large drums containing flammable or toxic substances?

2. What was the difference between a 'red lamp' establishment and a 'blue lamp'?

3. What would be referred to as Mutt and Jeff?

4. If the parapet of a trench faced the enemy, what is the name of the opposite, rear side of the trench?

5. Which three monarchs of countries fated to be at war were all first cousins?

6. What technique did artillery officer Brigadier-General Horne (later commander of the First Army) develop and use to high acclaim during the Battle of the Somme?

7. Which battle of October 1914, won by the Belgian Army allowed them to maintain a small territory and made King Albert a national hero?

8. On December 25 1914 an unofficial Christmas Truce was called at several points along the front lines which resulted in well documented fraternisation of troops. Where did the improbable 'football match' between the Argyll Highlanders and 133rd Saxon Regiment supposedly take place?

9. Who were referred to as the Pneumatic Cavalry?

10. What was the Jewel of Asia?

QUIZ 44 - BELGIUM

A selection of questions on Belgium's fate in the war:

1. Germany's offensive through neutral Belgium had the intention of taking control of Paris quickly, which other neutral country was invaded in the same action?

2. Started during the Battle of the Yser, near which city in West Flanders will you find the Dodengang (in Dutch), Le Boyau de la Mort (in French), the Trench of Death?

3. The German Army had a widescale policy of *Schrecklichkeit* whilst occupying Belgium. What was the intention of this policy?

4. The atrocities committed against the civilians and the wanton destruction of cultural establishments by the Germans in Belgium is often referred to as what?

5. Who was Belgium's Prime Minister during the war?

6. Where did Belgium's Government in exile operate from?

7. Who was the German military governor of Belgium from 1914 – 1917?

8. What was the 200 km long Dodendraad constructed along the Dutch-Belgium border?

9. They were dubbed King Albert's Heroes and saw action on the Eastern Front as well as being paraded in the United States. Who were they?

10. Why were the emergency houses – Drieduusters (three thousands), which sprang up after the war so named?

QUIZ 45 - GERMANY

Some questions on the Kaiser's country:

1. To whom did British Tommies refer to as Old One O' Clock?

2. What was the name of the German cruiser which caused havoc in the Indian and Pacific Oceans before finally being sunk by H.M.A.S. Sydney?

3. Germany's airships are often referred to as Zeppelins, however this just refers to those produced by the Zeppelin company, what was the name of the other major production company of airships?

4. Who was the commander of the German East Asia Squadron?

5. Who, on October 16 1915, became Germany's first air ace?

6. Whose plan was it to 'bleed France white' by launching a massive German attack at Verdun?

7. Who was seriously wounded on the Somme battlefield on October 7 1916 when a shell penetrated his dugout, killing several of his comrades and then was reputedly treated for his wounds in the crypt of Messines Church?

8. What was the name of the operation that resulted in Germany withdrawing their troops about 25 miles in March 1917, later known as the Hindenberg Line?

9. Manned by a crew of 18 and used in battle from March 1918, what were the A7V Sturmpanzerwagens Germany's versions of?

10. Which German commander described the first day of the Battle of Amiens in September 1918 as *The black day of the German Army*?

QUIZ 46 - NAME THE FILM

Identify the following films that are all based in or around World War One from these descriptions:

1. Starring Brad Pitt, Aidan Quinn and Anthony Hopkins, this epic family drama made in 1994 sees three brothers leave their home in Montana to join the Canadian Expeditionary Force and serve on the Western Front.

2. A Stanley Kubrick directed anti-war film of 1957 starring Kirk Douglas as a French colonel who defends his troops against accusations of cowardice.

3. A biographical film made in 2019 of a notable British author whose latter works of fantasy are highly influenced by his experiences on the Somme.

4. A 1966 film starring George Peppard as a German war ace on the Western Front.

5. A 1970 musical with lyrics by Johnny Mercer starring Julie Andrews and Rock Hudson about an English singer who is a German spy and her romance of an American pilot.

6. A David Lean directed film of 1970 which saw John Mills receive a supporting actor Oscar, it tells of a married Irish woman who has an affair with a British officer against the backdrop of the Easter Rising and the Great War.

7. Starring Daniel Craig and William Boyd this powerful drama from 1999 depicts the 48 hours leading up to the Battle of the Somme.

8. An early Mel Gibson film set around the experiences of a group of young Australians who enlist in the Australian army at the outbreak of war.

9. Released in 2019 this Sam Mendes directed film based in the trenches of northern France was critically acclaimed for its 'single shot' camera effect.

10. A 2017 fantasy film based around the exploits of a DC Comic's superhero and her efforts to thwart Ludendorff's creation of a deadlier form of mustard gas.

QUIZ 47 - TOMMIES' SLANG 2

What do the following slang terms that were used by the British Tommies translate to?

1. Butt-Notcher

2. San Fairy Ann

3. Camel Corps

4. Kiltie

5. Chatt

6. Mongey

7. Jugged

8 Emma Gee

9. Fairy Lights

10. Hard Tack

QUIZ 48 - THE BATTLE OF THE SOMME

A selection of questions on the battle that saw the worst day in British military history:

1. In which region of France is the Somme battlefield?

2. The main area of the battlefield was bisected by a straight Roman road, which two towns does it connect?

3. What was unique about the attack on High Wood on July 14 1916?

4. With which unit was American poet Alan Seeger serving when he was killed on the first day of the offensive whilst attacking the village of Belloy-en-Santerre?

5. A shallow depression south of the village of La Boiselle in the middle of the battlefield was nicknamed 'Sausage Valley' because of a German observation balloon stationed there. What nickname was given to a similar valley north of La Boiselle?

6. What was the name given to the German stronghold on Thiepval Ridge which became an insurmountable objective for the 36th (Ulster) Division on the first day?

7. Which captain of the Royal Army Medical Corps won a Victoria Cross at Guillemont on August 15 1916, for seeking out, and attending to, wounded men whilst under heavy fire?

8. Which future Prime Minister was badly wounded in a dawn attack at Lesboeufs on September 15 1916 then supposedly spent eight hours in a muddy shell-hole reading 'Prometheus Bound' in the original Greek?

9. What weapon was used for the first time in combat history at Flers in the eastern part of the Somme battlefield on September 15th, 1916?

10. Why did the Newfoundland Regiment begin their attack from the St. John's Road support trench, located behind their own front line?

QUIZ 49 - WOMEN AT WAR

Ten questions on the multitude of roles of women during the war.

1. During the war the 'marriage bar' was lifted (it was reinstated after the war), what did this mean?

2. In Britain, to the nearest 100,000 how many women joined the labour-force during the war?

3. Winning a Distinguished Service Medal for her outstanding work as Chief Operator of the U.S. Signal Corps' women telephone operators, what was the name of this outstanding servicewoman?

4. What was the name of the English journalist who disguised herself as a male soldier and became the only known English woman to have served in a military capacity on the frontlines during the war?

5. What is the name of the nurse who was killed during the Battle of Passchendaele and is buried at Lijssenthoek Military Cemetery?

6. Which New Zealand woman established a Volunteer Sisterhood that sent women from New Zealand to Egypt to care for New Zealand soldiers. After seeing the prevalence of venereal disease among the soldiers, she proposed the issuing of prophylactic kits which was adopted by the New Zealand Expeditionary Force at the end of 1917?

7. Nicknamed 'Ginger' because of her flaming red hair she is immortalised as a glittering statue in Poperinge town square, but what is the real name of the young girl who charmed all the officers at the cafe 'A la Poupee'?

8. The first woman to lead a Russian military unit was called Maria Bochareva who had petitioned the tsar for permission to join the Imperial Army in 1914. What was the name given to the battalion that she led?

9. Flora Sandes was the only British woman to serve as an official soldier during the war, though not in the British army, with which army did she serve as an officer?

10. In 1918 the Representation of the People Act gave certain women the right to vote. Which women were eligible?

QUIZ 50 - IT'S A DATE 2

More dates to name:

1. When did the first British Expeditionary Force troops land in France?

2. On what date was the Lusitania sunk?

3. On what date did Hauptmann Linnarz conduct the first Zeppelin bombing raid on London, killing seven and causing approximately £18,000 worth of damage?

4. On what date did the Germans commence the Battle of Verdun?

5. On what date did Britain and France secretly sign the Sykes-Picot Agreement which divided up the Middle East on the defeat of the Ottoman Empire?

6. On what date did the United States sever diplomatic relations with Germany?

7. On what date did British intelligence intercept the Zimmermann Telegram?

8. On what date did Russia sign an Armistice with Germany?

9. On what date did Germany start it's last great offensive of the war?

10. On what date were American forces victorious in the Battle of Cantigny, their first independent operation?

QUIZ 51 - TAKE IT EASY

Take a breather with some more, less challenging questions:

1. Where is Great Britain's Unknown Warrior buried?

2. Which fictional character, made famous on film by Harrison Ford, supposedly served in a Belgian unit on the Somme in 1916 and was subsequently taken prisoner by the Germans?

3. Beginning in the last months of the war, what caused the deaths of between 20 million and 50 million people worldwide?

4. What was the term given to the period when all soldiers in the trenches were required to shoulder arms in preparation of a possible German attack - especially just before dawn and nightfall?

5. Who led the Russian Revolution of 1917 which would ultimately result in armistice on the Eastern Front?

6. What was ANZAC an abbreviation for?

7. What was the name of the German offensive plan that entailed attacking France via neutral Belgium?

8. Who was the King of Great Britain throughout the war?

9. On what date did the Battle of the Somme commence?

10. What treaty officially brought the war between Germany and the Allies to an end?

QUIZ 52 - FOR THE EXPERTS ONLY!

Some questions for the real experts…..

1. Over which border region did fighting break out between Poland and Ukraine at the end of the war?

2. What was the date that the Canadians first saw action in the Battle of Passchendaele?

3. Who were the Turcos?

4. Formed in 1871 what was the German term for the Imperial German Navy?

5. Who wrote in The Morning Post on June 22 1915: *However the world pretends to divide itself, there are only two divisions in the world today – human beings and Germans.*?

6. On August 23 1914 which country declared war on Germany?

7. Charging a series of machine gun posts at Valenciennes and subsequently capturing the positions and the weapons, who was the last Canadian VC winner of the war?

8. Of which battle did General Henry Rawlinson describe the Australian advances as *the greatest achievement of the war*?

9. On what date were aircraft first used in the war?

10. Who, in 1909 prophetically proclaimed *The sky is about to become another battlefield no less important than the battlefields on land and sea ... In order to conquer the air, it is necessary to deprive the enemy of all means of flying, by striking at him in the air, at his bases of operation, or at his production centres. We had better get accustomed to this idea, and prepare ourselves.*?

QUIZ 53 - ARMY SIGNALLER'S CODE 2

For a private in the British Army of the Great War, what were the Army Signaller's code words for the following letters:

1. Y

2. B

3. K

4. P

5. V

6. E

7. H

8. Z

9. I

10. U

QUIZ 54 - GENERAL KNOWLEDGE 6

Yet another selection of general knowledge questions on the Great War to tax you:

1. What was the 'Soldier's Friend'?

2. What was considered as the most lethal form of poison gas used during the war?

3. A Bavarian duchess by birth, what was the name of the Belgium king's spouse during the war?

4. What did the troops commonly refer to as 'Plum Puddings'?

5. What is the official motto of the Royal Air Force?

6. What plant or flower holds special significance on Anzac Day?

7. Who was the last surviving combat soldier from any country to have fought in the Great War?

8. In which Belgian town during the war could be found the officers' restaurant named Skindles?

9. What three initials were stamped on the standard ration rum jars distributed amongst British companies?

10. From the hindustani word for bandage, what is the name of the strip of cloth that was wound round soldiers' legs from the top of the boot to the knee?

QUIZ 55 - INVENTORS AND INVENTIONS

Some questions on the inventors and inventions that came to the fore during the war.

1. What nationality was the prodigious aircraft designer Anthony Fokker?

2. What did John L Brodie design which became the first of its kind to be used by British troops in October 1915?

3. In 1914 Kimberly-Clark trademarked a product made from processed wood pulp named Cellucotton, which being five times more absorbent than cotton was sold to the American military for surgical dressing. However, after the war the company rebranded it and sold it as what?

4. As the British military attempted to find harder alloys for their guns, what did metallurgists discover by adding chromium to molten iron?

5. Interned on the Isle of Man as an enemy alien for more than three years during the war, a German bodybuilder developed a muscle strengthening regimen that he termed 'contrology'. What do we know this form of exercise as today?

6. Though women had been using them with straps as fashion accessories well before the war, what did men take out of their pockets and attach to their wrists during the conflict?

7. Which English born medical scientist, whilst working with the US Army Medical Corps on the Western Front effectively invented the blood bank?

8. What did Gideon Sundback perfect during the war that were initially used for money belts by soldiers and sailors who didn't have enough uniform pockets?

9. Kimberly-Clark continued to experiment with Cellucotton and created a thin, flattened version for gas mask filters. After the war they launched the product as a disposable makeup remover, but after customer feedback they changed them into what?

10. For what was future German Chancellor awarded a patent By King George V on June 26 1918?

QUIZ 56 - THE NEW ZEALANDERS

Ten questions on the role of the New Zealanders during the First World War:

1. What affectionate term, which remains today, referred to New Zealand soldiers?

2. What was the first act of the New Zealand Expeditionary Force?

3. In which country did the New Zealand soldiers, along with the Australians do their training before embarking on the ships that transported them to Gallipoli?

4. Born in Lewisham in Kent but emigrating to New Zealand in 1880, who was the highly regarded commander of the Wellington Infantry Battalion of the New Zealand Expeditionary Force, who was killed leading them at the Battle of Chunuk Blair on August 8 1915?

5. From which cemetery in Northern France was the New Zealand Unknown Soldier taken, who is now buried in the Wellington Memorial Park?

6. What name was given to the Otago Regiment after almost 200 of them died on New Zealand's bloodiest day in October 1917?

7. How many Victoria Crosses were awarded to New Zealand military personnel during the First World War?

8. What is unique about the Victoria Cross awarded to Auckland born Lieutenant Commander William Edward Sanders?

9. When did the New Zealand soldiers start to return home en masse to New Zealand after the war?

10. What incredible percentage of New Zealand men served during the war?

QUIZ 57 - THE HOME FRONT

Some things went on as normal in Britain during the war, other things did not. Answer these questions on life away from the front lines:

1. Who starred and directed 1915's film *In The Park*?

2. Who was the British flat racing Champion Jockey in every year of the war?

3. Known as the 'Khaki Cup Final', who won the 1915 F.A. Cup Final?

4. Which popular music hall star and comedian, who wrote and performed 'Roamin in the Gloamin' raised huge sums for the war effort by performing and travelling throughout the British Empire?

5. Known as 'The Great White Hope', who knocked out Jack Johnson in April 1915 to become the Heavyweight Boxing World Champion?

6. In 1917 King George V changed the family name to Windsor. What was it prior to this?

7. The bestselling book in Britain in 1917 was entitled *Mr Britling Sees It Through*, who was the British author?

8. In 1917 in Memphis, Tennessee the blues was becoming an established and popular music form. In that year whose work entitled Beale Street Blues was published?

9. In which year did David Lloyd George take over as Prime Minister from Herbert Asquith?

10. In 1917 two cousins took five extraordinary photographs near their home in Bradford. They soon caught the public's imagination and had support from Arthur Conan Doyle. What fantastic phenomenon did they depict?

QUIZ 58 - IT'S A GENERAL THING

Answer these questions on a few of the notable military generals of the war:

1. Which outstanding Australian General was commander of the 4th Infantry Brigade in Gallipoli, and in May 1918 became the commander of the Australian Corps - the largest individual corps on the Western Front at the time?

2. Which lieutenant general was the senior leader of British military aviation during the war, serving as commander of the RFC in the field and later was instrumental in establishing the RAF as an independent body?

3. This man was a hugely successful German general who caused massive casualties on the Russians at the Battle of Tannenburg. He was appointed Chief of the General Staff in 1916 and after the war became President of the German Reich. Who was he?

4. Which incompetent general repeatedly ordered attacks against the Turks holding the hill of Achi Baba in May 1915 causing 6000 casualties to his men and gaining just 600 yards in three days but failing to secure the objective?

5. Though British born he is regarded as New Zealand's most famous soldier. He took part in the beach landings at Gallipoli, was the youngest general in the British Army in the war, won the Victoria Cross and three Distinguished Service Orders, then served New Zealand as the 7th Governor-General from 1946 – 1952. Name him!

6. Which German general commanded and advised the Ottoman military at Gallipoli?

7. Given the nickname 'Bloody Bull' he served with the BEF on the Western Front and later led the British Empire's Egyptian Expeditionary Force during the Sinai and Palestine Campaign against the Ottoman Empire in the conquest of Palestine. In 1919 he was made a Field Marshal, Viscount and Governor of Egypt. What was his name?

8. Who commanded the Canadians Corps who would finally get to liberate Passchendaele?

9. Who was the Russian Imperial Army's Commander-in-Chief at the beginning of the war until the Gorlice-Tarnow Offensive of 1915 when he was removed?

10. Which British Army officer commanded V Corps at the Second Battle of Ypres in April 1915, took command of the Second Army in May 1915 and in June 1917 won an overwhelming victory over the German Army at the Battle of Messines. Later he served as Commander-in-Chief of the British Army of the Rhine and after the war as Governor of Malta?

QUIZ 59 - INITIALLY SPEAKING 2

The following initials would have been familiar abbreviations during the Great War. What are they short for?

1. C.E.F.

2. D.F.C.

3. A.O.C.

4. Q.M.G.

5. G.O.C.

6. H.B.M.G.C.

7. R.N.D.

8. A.C.C.

9. B.W.M.

10. A.E.F.

QUIZ 60 - CURRENCY AFFAIRS

What was the chief currency of these Great War belligerents during the war?

1. Canada

2. France

3. Austria-Hungary

4. Russia

5. Japan

6. Germany

7. Ottoman Empire

8. Australia

9. India

10. German East Africa

QUIZ 61 - WHO SAID THAT?

Identify who made these following statements:

1. Commenting on the Serbian response to Austria-Hungary's ultimatum of 1914, who said: *A great moral victory for Vienna, but with it, every reason for war disappears*?

2. Which former and future Australian Prime Minister said in early August 1914: *Should the worst happen Australia would rally to the Mother Country to help and defend her to our last man and our last shilling*?

3. Which senior French commander stated: *If the women in the factories stopped work for twenty minutes, the Allies would lose the war*?

4. *This war, like the next war, is a war to end war* was said by which British Prime Minister?

5. Which newspaper owner who lost three sons during the First World War said: *We're telling lies; we know we're telling lies; we don't tell the public the truth, that we're losing more officers than the Germans, and that it's impossible to get through on the Western Front*?

6. Who prophetically said after the signing of the Treaty of Versailles: *This is not a peace. It is an armistice for 20 years.*?

7. On November 11 1918 who proclaimed: *At eleven o'clock this morning came to an end the cruellest and most terrible war that has ever scourged mankind. I hope we may say that thus, this fateful morning came to an end all wars.*?

8. Which British politician said on the eve of war: *The lamps are going out all over Europe, we shall not see them lit again in our life-time.*?

9. American President Woodrow Wilson said: *This is a war to end all wars.* But he didn't invent the statement. Who did?

10. Who countered Woodrow Wilson's statement by saying: *Only the dead have seen the end of war*?

QUIZ 62 - ANAGRAMS 6

Decipher the following anagrams to reveal another place associated with the Great War:

1. A Palmolive Therim

2. Glam Karen

3. Soho Lego Ellen

4. Amorous Daunts You

5. Ivy Grimed

6. Archangel Carrot

7. Mowed Matzo

8. Singers Demise

9. Behold Hunter Lorenzo

10. Leaded Snarl

QUIZ 63 - GENERAL KNOWLEDGE 7

Another general knowledge selection of questions:

1. The ending of which battle also finished the race to the sea as the Allies prevented the Germans from reaching Calais or Dunkirk?

2. What was the famous slogan on the British recruitment poster and advertisement of 1914 that encouraged so many men to join the armed services?

3. What was the difference between 'male' British tanks and 'female'?

4. The Tommies in the trenches were particularly familiar with one brand of jam, what was it?

5. He was one of the most decorated American serviceman of the war, receiving a Medal of Honor for leading an attack on a German machine gun nest, taking at least one machine gun, killing at least 25 enemy soldiers and capturing 132. Who was he?

6. Which soldier poet wrote the poem *Anthem For Doomed Youth*?

7. What term in the Indian Army was given to an infantry private soldier?

8. How was Geoffrey Studdert Kennedy better known?

9. Standing just 4 feet 9 inches tall who was the shortest corporal in the British Army?

10. In 1915 a new style of fashion for women was popularised whereby they would wear very full, calf-length skirts. What was this fashion nicknamed?

QUIZ 64 - IT'S ALL ABOUT THE NUMBERS 2

All the answers are numbers ......

1. How many Victoria Crosses were awarded during the war?

2. Of the approximately 800 Newfoundlanders who went into battle on the first day of the Somme how many were at roll call the next morning?

3. For how many days did the Third Battle of Ypres (Passchendaele) last?

4. When conscription was introduced in Britain it was for men aged between 18 and 40, the age limit was later raised to what age?

5. What's the number of tanks that were produced by Germany during the war?

6. How many principles of peace did Woodrow Wilson have?

7. What's the number of forts facing the German army when they attacked Verdun in February 1916?

8. Officially, what was the age you had to have attained to serve in the British Army overseas?

9. In the Battle of Jutland 151 British warships faced how many German ships?

10. What's the number of VCs won by Australians in the First World War?

QUIZ 65 - INDIA

Ten questions on the importance of India during the Great War:

1. When did the first contingent of Indian soldiers (Indian Expeditionary Force A) arrive in France?

2. Born in India in 1857 who commanded the Indian Corps in France in 1914?

3. Which Indian soldier became the first recipient of the Victoria Cross for his actions at Hollebeke in Belgium during the First Battle of Ypres on October 31 1914?

4. How many expeditionary forces were formed and dispatched overseas by the Indian Army in the war?

5. A soldier holding the rank of subedar in the Indian Army would have what equivalent rank in the British Army?

6. During the war how many Indian soldiers won Victoria Crosses?

7. Which great Indian advocator of peace, supported Britain's war efforts throughout, and whilst in England in August 1914 helped to raise an Indian ambulance corps?

8. To the nearest one hundred thousand, how many Indians served in the Great War, as either combatants or non-combatants?

9. In which battle on the Western Front where they fought nearly to the last man, did James Willcocks proclaim that the Ghurkas had found their Valhalla?

10. In 2011 an Indian Forces Memorial was unveiled on the ramparts by the south side of the Menin Gate, however before then there was only one memorial to this country's great contribution to the war effort. Where is this memorial?

QUIZ 66 - BATTLE OF ARRAS

A selection of questions on the Battle of Arras:

1. On what date did the Battle of Arras commence?

2. Intended to take German reserves away from the French lines on the Aisne and the Chemin des Dames, the Battle of Arras was the first part of which Offensive, named after its French proponent?

3. Which sergeant, already a Military Medal recipient for his actions in 1916, was awarded a Victoria Cross for his actions on April 9 1917 when under heavy fire, succeeded in reaching the enemy trench alone, subsequently killed an entire machine-gun team and officer and then held the end of the trench with such effect that a bombing squad were able to capture 100 prisoners and five machine-guns?

4. The taking of which ridge by the Canadian Corps was seen as an early great victory?

5. Which British general, leading the Third Army devised the plan and was told by Haig that any failures would be his responsibility?

6. Which professional footballer for both Manchester City (110 appearances) and Manchester United (220 appearances) who scored 143 first class goals and the first goal at Old Trafford in February 1909 was killed during the Battle of Arras May 3 1917 aged 32?

7. The Royal Flying Corps had an important role in the Battle of Arras, particularly in reconnaissance and bombing. Who was the strident commander of the Corps at the time?

8. Which German general, commanding the 6th Army at Arras was removed by Ludendorff after the battle and became a governor-general of Belgium until the end of the war, presiding over 170 executions of Belgian civilians?

9. In which sector of the Arras battlefield did the Australian Imperial Force fight two gruelling battles on April 11 and May 3 that incurred great losses for which Monash would write *our men are being put into the hottest fighting and are being sacrificed in hair-brained ventures* ?

10. On what date did the Battle of Arras officially end?

QUIZ 67 - WORLD LEADERS 2

At the beginning of the Great War who were the following world leaders?

1. The Canadian Prime Minister

2. The President of France

3. President of Portugal

4. The Prime Minister of New Zealand

5. Prime Minister of South Africa

6. Prime Minister of Romania

7. Prime Minister of Serbia

8. Prime Minister of Luxembourg

9. Emperor of Austria-Hungary

10. King of Greece

QUIZ 68 - WHAT'S THE REAL NAME? 2

What were the proper names of the towns and villages that the Tommies referred to as the following:

1. Vlam

2. Roody Boys

3. Doing it

4. Funky Villas

5. Hazybrook

6. Hop Out

7. Jolly Polly

8. Ruin

9. Lousy Wood

10. Ocean Villas

QUIZ 69 - A QUESTION OF SPORT

The following notable sportsmen all tragically lost their lives in the Great War. For which sports were they renowned?

1. Jack Harrison VC MC, East Yorkshire Regiment, killed Oppy Wood, France on May 3 1917.

2. Ronald Poulton, Royal Berkshire Regiment, shot by an enemy sniper May 5 1915 repairing a trench near Ploegsteert Wood.

3. Arthur Montague Septimus Jones, serving in the 8th Australian Light Horse Regiment, killed ay Gallipoli August 7 1915.

4. New Zealander Tony Wilding, captain in the Royal Naval Armoured Car division, killed in action during the Battle of Aubers Ridge May 9 1915.

5. Publican Henry Berry from Gloucester in England who served with the Gloucestershire Regiment. Killed in action May 9 1915 at Aubers Ridge.

6. Second-Lieutenant Donald Simpson Bell VC, a teacher from Harrogate who joined the West Yorkshire Regiment in 1915. He was awarded his VC for actions on July 5 1915 at Horseshoe Trench on the Somme. He was shot by a sniper on July 10 1916 attacking a machine gun post near Contalmaison.

7. Canadian Francis (Frank) McGee, though bling in one eye he had a notable sports career and served in the Canadian Army, killed in action September 16 1916 near Courcelette.

8. Frederick Septimus Kelly, an Olympian from the London Olympics of 1908 who was born in Sydney but served with the Royal Naval Division. Wounded twice at Gallipoli and awarded the DSO, he was killed at Beaucourt-sur-l'Ancre rushing a German machine gun post on November 13 1916.

9. Edgar Roberts 'Mobbsy' Mobbs, Lieutenant Colonel in the Northamptonshire Regiment who was killed on the opening day of the Third Battle of Ypres at Pilckem Ridge aged 35. His body was never found and he was posthumously awarded the DSO.

10. Born in Deptford in Kent, Englishman Colin (aka Charlie) Blythe served with the King's Own Yorkshire Light Infantry in the Ypres Salient where he was killed near Passchendaele by shrapnel whilst working on a railway line.

QUIZ 70 - NAME THE AUTHOR

Who wrote the following novels that were based during or around the Great War?

1. All Quiet On The Western Front

2. Birdsong

3. War Horse

4. A Farewell To Arms

5. The Return of the Soldier

6. Parade's End

7. Regeneration

8. The Camels Are Coming

9. A Long Long Way

10. The Good Soldier Svejk

QUIZ 71 – THE GREAT WAR IN AFRICA

The First World War represented a pivotal point in Africa's history. Try answering these questions on the war on that continent:

1. What was the official name given to the colonial troops in the African territories of the German Colonial Empire?

2. Which strategic body of water saw the British motorboats HMS Mimi and Toutou defeat the two German warships Hedwig von Wissmann and Kingani?

3. Killed on August 22 1914 whilst commanding a force of French Senegalese troops during the Togoland Campaign, who was the first British officer to be killed in action during the First World War?

4. In which battle of September 26 1914 were German forces victorious against the Union of South Africa fighting on behalf of the British Imperial Government?

5. Who was the South African Defence Minister – a former Second Boer War general, who actively supported South Africa's joining of the Allies against Germany in the war?

6. With which European forces, with whom it was not officially at war, did Germany clash in its campaign in Angola between October 1914 – July 1915?

7. Who was the last, and defeated, German commander of the Kamerun Campaign?

8. Throughout the First World War and into 1921 French troops were involved in the Zaian War against Berber tribes in which North African country?

9. What was the name of the uprising in Nyasaland against British colonialism in January 1915 led by a Baptist minister that was motivated by the harsh treatments imposed in the indigenous population?

10. Who was the last German commander to surrender?

QUIZ 72 - ANAGRAMS 7

And some more anagrams to decipher - this time to reveal the name of a person associated with the Great War:

1. Brisk Leila

2. Agnes Coerce Legume

3. Larruping Kiddy

4. Falsehood Scavengery

5. Below Oiled Wini

6. GP Henri Johns

7. Enzymic Bald Alf

8. Trickled Heron

9. America Require Harm

10. Provincial Prig

QUIZ 73 - GENERAL KNOWLEDGE 8

Yet more general knowledge questions:

1. Who was the leader of the Labour Party, and future Prime Minister, who resigned his position in 1914 due to his opposition of the war?

2. What is the iron harvest?

3. Who was the Founder President of the British Legion (later Royal British Legion)?

4. Which General first suggested the idea of 'Pals Battalions' by appealing to London stockbrokers to raise a battalion from workers in the City of London?

5. Who was the only soldier to be awarded the Victoria Cross twice during the Great War?

6. The carriage that brought the body of the Unknown Warrior back to Britain is known as the Cavell Van because it had already repatriated the body of Edith Cavell. However, what was the name of the third person, killed in the war, whose body was repatriated in the van?

7. Why was conscription not introduced in Ireland?

8. What did the initials W.W.C.S. stand for?

9. What were the four main gases used as weapons during the war?

10. What was the Balfour Declaration made by Britain in 1917?

QUIZ 74 - VISITING THE WAR SITES TODAY

A selection of questions of a more contemporary feel, examining the war sites as you might visit them today:

1. At what time every night do the buglers play The Last Post at the Menin Gate?

2. The fascinating Carriere Wellington Tunnels which hid thousands of allied soldiers during the war can be visited by going to which French town?

3. In which town in the Somme region of France will you find the impressive *Historial de la Grande Guerre* museum?

4. The Spanbroekmolen Mine Crater or Lone Tree Crater which was the result of the largest of the 19 mines detonated on June 7 1917 is now known as what?

5. A wonderfully preserved example of the fortifications at Verdun that is open to the public, what is it called?

6. An impressive and authentic example of landscape and preserved trenches from the war can be seen in a park near to Beaumont Hamel on the Somme, what is the name of the park?

7. The In Flanders Fields museum can be found in the rebuilt Cloth Hall in which iconic town?

8. Suitably named, this is one of Turkey's top ten tourist attractions with several poignant memorials and an annual commemoration on April 25, what is it called?

9. Overlooking the River Marne, this monument, sometimes known as the Hill 204 Monument, commemorates those American soldiers who fought in the region during the Great War, what is it?

10. Where would you find the delightful Ocean Villas Tea Rooms?

QUIZ 75 - THE AUSTRALIANS

Some questions on the role of the Australians:

1. Which ship, operated by a German shipping company became the target of the first shot fired by Australian forces in the war as it ventured to leave the port of Melbourne on August 5 1914?

2. In which Australian state were the first four battalions of the 1st Australian Division raised?

3. What was the Australian 5th Battalion also known as?

4. From what bird did the feathers in the slouch hats of the soldiers of the Australian Light Horse come?

5. Who was the Australian Prime Minister at the start of the war?

6. Which attack in July 1916 saw Australia's debut on the Western Front?

7. Which village on the Somme did the Australian 1st Division take on July 23 1916, the ridge nearby being described by the official historian as being "more densely sown with Australian sacrifice than any other place on earth."?

8. For his actions in Gallipoli who was the first Australian to be awarded a Victoria Cross, and who would later be awarded and MV and bar?

9. What was the affectionate name given to Australian soldiers derived both from mining in their home country and for constructing trenches during the war?

10. What was the name of the only Australian pilot to be awarded a Victoria Cross in WW1?

QUIZ 76 - VIVE LA FRANCE

Ten questions to tax your knowledge of the French experiences in the Great War:

1. In September 1914 how were the French soldiers from the Paris Garrison allegedly transported to the Battle of the Marne?

2. What nickname was given to the Battle of Verdun by Crown Prince William?

3. Which French pilot was the first fighter ace in history before being shot down and killed on August 31 1915 at Petit-Croix, France?

4. Who was in overall command of the French armies fighting in the southern sectors of the Somme battlefield between July and November 1916?

5. Who replaced General Robert Nivelle as Commander in Chief of the French Armies after the failed Nivelle Offensive?

6. Which future leader of France was wounded multiple times, decorated for his extensive examples of bravery and a company commander at Verdun before being captured by the Germans and finishing the war as a prisoner of war though he made five unsuccessful escape attempts?

7. What type of rifle was mainly used by the French infantry throughout the First World War?

8. What were the Zouaves?

9. To the nearest ten thousand, how many French soldiers were killed at the Battle of Verdun?

10. Which French aviator finished the war as the top Entente fighter ace with 75 confirmed victories (of which 3 were shared)?

QUIZ 77 - ALL AT SEA 2

Another set of questions on the naval conflict:

1. Which Australian submarine, commanded by Lieutenant-Commander Henry Stoker, caused havoc in the Sea of Marmara in April 1915 as part of the Gallipoli Campaign before eventually being scuttled by its crew?

2. What did Admiral Ludwig von Reuter do to the German Fleet whilst at the Royal Navy's base at Scapa Flow in the Orkney Islands on June 21 1919?

3. On February 16 1918, HMHS Glenart Castle was sunk by a German U-boat. What did the initials 'HMHS' stand for?

4. October 26-27 1916 saw the Germans achieve an important victory through their use of torpedo boats. What was the name of the battle?

5. The Germans conducted a raid on Dover Strait in April 1917, during which German and British crews were reported to have engaged in which old-fashioned act of naval warfare?

6. Which future king of Great Britain saw action as a sub-lieutenant in the Battle of Jutland?

7. In 1917 which country's navy did Britain call upon to help tackle the German and Austria-Hungarian submarines operating in the Mediterranean Sea?

8. Which was the first Anglo-Japanese operation of the war when a German port in China was taken siege by their two navies?

9. Taking place between May 14-15 1917 what was the largest surface action in the Adriatic Sea during the war?

10. Aged 16 who was the youngest recipient of the VC during the Great War being awarded it for his actions on board HMS Chester during the Battle of Jutland when though fatally wounded he refused to leave his post for the duration of the battle?

QUIZ 78 - NAME THE BATTLE 2

Some more battles for you to identify by these simple descriptions:

1. This battle proved to be a hugely destructive victory by Germany on Russia at the end of August 1914.

2. A naval engagement on January 24 1915 in which the British Grand Fleet surprised and defeated German ships in the North Sea.

3. Taking place between 10-13 March 1915 this was the first British initiated offensive of the war.

4. Commencing on August 27 1916 this was the first major operation of the Romanian Forces in the war and although they were defeated by the Central Powers it did help to halt the German offensive at Verdun.

5. Fought between July 31 - August 2 1917 this was the opening battle of the Third Battle of Ypres.

6. Sometimes referred to as the Twelfth Battle of the Isonzo, this battle was a resounding success for the Central Powers in Italy in October 1917 causing approximately 300,000 casualties to the Allied Powers.

7. This battle on October 23 1917 was a resounding success for the French on the Chemin des Dames, advancing 6 km, securing 180 guns and taking 11,157 prisoners.

8. Occurring on October 27 1917, the 8th Mounted Brigade of the Egyptian Expeditionary Force repelled an infantry and cavalry attack by the Yildrim Army Group of the Ottoman Empire.

9. The only tank versus tank battle of the war taking place on April 24 1918.

10. In Canada's last hundred days, the battle where 7 Victoria Crosses won.

QUIZ 79 - THIRD BATTLE OF YPRES

Ten questions on the brutal Third Battle of Ypres.

1. In what country is Passchendaele?

2. On what date did the Third Battle of Ypres start?

3. At what time did the British launch the first attack of the battle on the Germans at Pilckem Ridge?

4. Who was the overall commander of the Allied offensive in the campaign to liberate Passchendaele?

5. General Hubert Gough, one of the commanders in the battle, was the inspiration of a sect of officers to form a group called 'GMG'. What did these initials stand for?

6. After Viscount Plumer took over from Gough in the battle he paused the offensive for three weeks, why?

7. September 20-25 saw Plumer's first offensive since taking charge and he used twice as many pieces of artillery. What was the name of the battle?

8. Assaulting Bellevue Spur on October 12 which country suffered their most horrific day in their military history with an estimated 957 dead?

9. Which actual Canadian battalion captured Passchendaele on November 6 1917?

10. The numbers: the battle took over three months, utilised 50 British and Empire divisions, 6 French Divisions and fought against 83 divisions. To the nearest ten thousand, how many casualties are there estimated to have been?

QUIZ 80 - TOMMIES' SLANG 3

What do the following slang terms that were used by the British Tommies translate to?

1. Jam-Tins

2. Chuck a dummy

3. The Byng Boys

4. Kip-shop

5. Look Stick

6. Minnie

7. Croaker

8. Mufti

9. Napoo

10. Pork and Beans

QUIZ 81 - MORE FILMS

Identify the following films that are all based during or around World War One from these descriptions:

1. The first film that Charlie Chaplin directed, it sees the Little Tramp serving in France where he not only captures thirteen Germans by 'surrounding them', but also captures the Kaiser and Crown Prince.

2. King Vidor's epic tale of the Great War and the biggest financial success of the silent era.

3. A notoriously expensive Howard Hughes film released in 1930 famous for its flying sequences.

4. Starring Boris Karloff and Victor McLaglen this John Ford film from 1934 tells of a company of men trying to find a w ay out of the Mesopotamia desert.

5. A Howard Hawks directed film from 1936 starring Fredric March and Warner Baxter, this is a dramatic and dark tale of the Great War.

6. Mario Monicelli's cinematic masterpiece from 1959 which won the Venice Film Festival Golden Lion, this follows two Italian soldiers on the Austrian Front who try to shirk any and all responsibility.

7. Dirk Bogarde and Tom Courtenay star in this bleak 1964 film about a deserter being tried by a trench tribunal.

8. Richard Attenborough's directorial debut in 1969, a comedy musical based on the stage musical of the same name.

9. A multilingual 2005 drama looking at the Christmas truce of 1914 through the eyes of Scottish, French and German soldiers.

10. A 2008 Canadian made film based around the Third Battle of Ypres which contains little of historic value.

QUIZ 82 - ANAGRAMS 8

Decipher the following anagrams to reveal the name of another person associated with the Great War:

1. Renounce Libyan

2. Wow! Indoor Owls

3. Reefy Flamingos

4. Hurdler Coffined

5. Reinfects a rhubarb

6. Looser Neglige

7. Volgograd Yielded

8. Jeff Jr Poohes

9. For Jenn Hirsch

10. Holt Hulk Movement

QUIZ 83 - GENERAL KNOWLEDGE 9

Round 9 of general knowledge questions on the Great War for you to get your teeth into!

1. Which country joined the Triple Entente in August 1916 after the signing of the Treaty of Bucharest?

2. What nickname was given to those of the American Signal Corps Female Telephone Operators Unit?

3. Containing such things as chocolate and tobacco, the serving troops in Christmas 1914 were given a small brass box gift. It was funded largely by the public but was inspired by which royal?

4. Although the wearing of these were abandoned shortly after reaching Britain in 1914, the Newfoundland regiment were given a nickname after a part of the uniform. What was the nickname?

5. What caused trench fever among the troops?

6. What did the Germans call the Hindenberg Line?

7. Which writer, poet and second lieutenant in the Royal Welch Fusilier, known as 'Mad Jack' to his men for his apparently suicidal exploits, won a Military Cross for raiding the German trench lines at Fricourt?

8. Regarded as commencing in April 1915, against whom did the Ottoman Empire commit a mass genocide which lasted throughout the war and on until 1923?

9. Who wrote the music and lyrics to *Keep The Home Fires Burning*?

10. With which army did the Ghurkas fight during the war?

QUIZ 84 - IN MEMORIAM

Some questions remembering the human cost of the war:

1. Who was the founder of the Imperial War Graves Commission?

2. Which is the largest British Military Cemetery in the World?

3. Who designed the Menin Gate Memorial to the Missing?

4. Sir Reginald Blomfield's Cross of Sacrifice incorporating a bronze longsword is found in Commonwealth War Graves Cemeteries containing how many graves?

5. There are 54,389 names of officers and men from Britain and Commonwealth Forces who fell in the Ypres Salient before August 16 1917 and have no known grave. Two Commonwealth forces are not represented, which are they?

6. Where will you find the Tomb of the Unknown Australian Soldier?

7. In what year was the Thiepval Memorial finally finished?

8. To the nearest thousand, how many names are on the Thiepval Memorial?

9. Who designed London's Cenotaph?

10. Who suggested the phrases *Known Unto God* inscribed on the gravestones of unidentified soldiers and *Their Name Liveth For Evermore* on the Stones of Remembrance in British Cemeteries?

QUIZ 85 - IT'S A DATE 3

Some more dates to identify:

1. On what date did Britain and France declare war on the Ottoman Empire?

2. On what date did Allied troops move through Mesopotamia to successfully capture Baghdad from the Ottoman Empire?

3. On what date was Serbia invaded by a combined force of Austria-Hungarian and German troops?

4. On what date was the 'Great Arab Uprising' when the Arab Nationalists led a revolt against the Ottoman rule?

5. On what date did the Battle of Verdun end?

6. On what date was the U.S. cargo ship SS Aztec sunk by Germany as it made its way to France?

7. On what date was General Pershing chosen as commander of the American Expeditionary Force?

8. On what date did the American Forces start to arrive in France?

9. On what date did Britain issue the Balfour Declaration?

10. On what date did the Allied forces commence the attack at Meuse-Argonne, which would become the final big offensive of the war?

QUIZ 86 - THE HISTORIANS 2

Who wrote these influential histories of the Great War?

1. Undertones of War (1928)

2. Forgotten Victory: The First World War - Myths and Realities (2001)

3. Old Soldiers Never Die (1933)

4. The War The Infantry Knew (1938)

5. 'Stand To' A Diary of the Trenches (1937)

6. Testament of Youth (1933)

7. An Onlooker in France (1921)

8. The First World War (1998 - Hutchinson)

9. Before Endeavours Fade (1976)

10. The Guns of August (1962)

QUIZ 87 - WHO AM I? 2

Some more famous people to identify from these descriptions:

1. I was born in an impressive family home in Woodstock, Oxfordshire and led an interesting and varied life. During the war I served both in the government and on the Western Front, but my real 'moment' wouldn't come until the dark days of the Second World War.

2. I first saw action in the Great War as a junior officer of the Royal Warwickshire Regiment. During the First Battle of Ypres I was shot through the right lung by a sniper but returned to the Western Front as a general staff officer. I took part in the battles of Arras and Passchendaele before finishing the war as Chief of Staff of the 47th (2nd London) Division. During the Second World War I would have few military superiors.

3. I was born on December 12 1885 in Maryborough, Queensland, Australia and found my calling when opening an Everyman's Club behind the lines which would provide a haven in hell for thousands of men.

4. I was born on December 30 1865 and became world famous for my writings, especially my jungle stories. Having felt the pain of losing my son John during the Battle of Loos I was instrumental in some of the terms being adopted that are familiar in Britain's military cemeteries.

5. I was born on October 2 1851 in Tarbes, France. As a 19 year old I served in the army in the Franco-Prussian war, but saw no combat. In the Great War I ultimately served as the Supreme Allied Commander.

6. In my own words 'I am enormously talented and there is no point in denying it'. I was an acclaimed English actor, playwright, composer, director and artist among other things and served in 1918 with the Artists Rifles but didn't see any action as I was invalided out with a tubercular problem.

7. I was born on June 3 1865 in London, then when I was only 12 I joined HMS Britannia in Dartmouth. Both my sons would play a part in the war and I made the judicial decision to change our family name.

8. I was born in Chorlton-on-Medlock, Manchester in 1863 but always considered myself a true Welshman. Welsh was my first language and to date I am the only Welshman to become Prime Minister of the United Kingdom, I was also the last Liberal to hold that position.

9. A German fighter ace of the war, I was awarded the 'Blue Max' and commanded for a short period in 1918 the Red Baron's famous fighter wing "Freiherr von Richthofen". In later years I would become commander in chief of the Luftwaffe before committing suicide in 1946.

10. I was born on August 3 1887 in Rugby, my fellow poet Yeats once said I was the handsomest young man in England. I rest in a corner of a foreign field, far from home in the Mediterranean, not the victim of a bullet but of an infected insect bite.

QUIZ 88 - NAME THE COUNTRY 2

Name the country in which the following cities, towns or villages, all familiar to Great War scholars, today reside:

1. Festubert

2. Diksmuide

3. Lodz

4. Krithia

5. Gorizia (or Goritz)

6. Zonnebeke

7. Kut (Kut-al-Amara)

8. Baku

9. Hulluch

10. Cheriton

QUIZ 89 - IT'S ALL UP IN THE AIR 2

Another selection of questions on the war in the air:

1. During the First Battle of the Marne how were aircraft principally used?

2. Approximately what was the top speed of the Great War fighter planes?

3. Which two organisations merged to form the Royal Air Force?

4. To become an air 'ace' how many victories did a pilot have to notch up?

5. How did Germany mark their aircraft?

6. What term did British pilots give to anti-aircraft guns?

7. What was the term given to fights between aircraft whilst airborne?

8. What type of heavy German bombers appeared in the skies over London for the first time on Wednesday 13 June 1917?

9. What term did pilots give to their attempts to down enemy observation balloons?

10. How many wings did the Fokker Dr.1 have?

QUIZ 90 – BEHIND ENEMY LINES

Some questions about those who found themselves, for one reason or another, behind the enemy lines:

1. Which trooper of the 11th Hussars became cut off from his regiment after the Battle of Le Cateau and after spending five months living in the woods was taken in by a French family, subsequently spending much of the rest of the war hiding in a cupboard?

2. Which French chateau saw the execution by the Germans of 11 British soldiers caught behind the lines after the retreat from Mons to the Marne and a local labourer named Chalandre who had helped to shelter them?

3. In pulling a German officer from his horse and riding away to safety, who is the only known condemned man to escape from a German firing squad?

4. Not exactly behind enemy lines, but where was the internment camp that for much of the war held 1500 men of the First Royal Naval Brigade under the command of Commodore Wilfred Henderson - the internees would refer to the camp as HMS Timbertown, whilst the locals as Engelse Kamp?

5. Escaping from Donington Hall Prisoner of War Camp in Leicestershire on July 4 1915, who would become the only person to ever escape from a British camp and return home safely?

6. What were the Mannschaftslager?

7. Which future Lieutenant-General competed in the 1924 Olympics, commanded XXX Corps at Operation Market Garden during the Second World War, was Black Rod at the House of Lords for fourteen years and a prisoner of the Germans during the Great War?

8. From which Turkish POW camp did Welshman Elias Henry Jones and Australian Cedric Waters Hill successfully escape by convincing their captors that they were insane?

9. Who was the future French Second World War General of the Free French Forces that escaped from a POW camp in Belgium in the First World War and by receiving help from Edith Cavell and Princess Marie of Croy amongst others was able to return to France via the Netherlands?

10. From which German POW camp did the 'Great Escape' take place on July 24 1918 in which 29 men escaped, 19 of them subsequently getting caught but with 10 of them reaching Holland?

QUIZ 91 - CHOOSE YOUR WEAPON

Answer these questions on Great War armaments:

1. What type of gas was used by the Germans against French Colonial troops near the St Juliaan Road in April 1915?

2. What did the Germans introduce to the battlefield at Hooge on July 30 1915?

3. Unveiled in September 1915 what was the name given to the first prototype tank?

4. Devised by Captain McClintock of the British Indian Army in 1912, what was the name given to the highly effective explosive charge placed within one or more connected tubes to clear obstacles such as mines, barbed wire and booby traps?

5. What was lyddite?

6. What were the Scene Shifter and Boche Busters?

7. Named after their inventor, what were the first type of hand grenades that were designed to fragment?

8. What invention by American soldier Isaac Newton-Lewis was used by the British, French and Belgian armies?

9. What was the standard calibre of the British Short Lee Enfield rifle?

10. What was the name of the unpopular Canadian rifle that was withdrawn from frontline action in 1916 but still used due to its exceptional accuracy by snipers until the end of the war?

QUIZ 92 - THE AMERICANS ARE COMING

Answer these ten questions on the involvement of the United States of America in the Great War:

1. On what date did the United States declare war on Germany?

2. Who was the Commander-in-Chief of the American Expeditionary Force?

3. What ship was sunk by Germany that is regarded as pivotal in bringing America into the war?

4. Which country was urged in the Zimmermann telegram to attack the United States?

5. Which American soldier poet wrote 'I Have A Rendez-vous With Death'?

6. What was the Housatonic?

7. Who was the first American pilot to be awarded the Medal of Honour and was regarded as their greatest 'balloon buster'?

8. On May 28 1918 American forces secured their first major victory, what was the battle?

9. At which battle did American marines stop the German army from crossing the Marne River in June 1918, the woods in the area being renamed after the war *Woods of the Marine Brigade*?

10. Who was the most famous of the 'Harlem Hellfighters' who France awarded the Croix de Guerre, and his own country, posthumously, the Purple Heart and Distinguished Service Cross.

QUIZ 93 - GENERAL KNOWLEDGE 10

And yet more questions of a general knowledge nature on the war to answer:

1. What was the Armenian Legion?

2. What is the name of the treaty, signed on August 10 1920 that officially ended the war between the Ottoman Empire and the Allies?

3. Many women took up employment in the munitions factories during the war where the conditions were often hazardous. Some of these women were subsequently given a nickname due to the colour that their skin had been turned from working with toxic chemicals. By what were they known?

4. What device did soldiers in the trenches use to safely see over the parapet and into No Man's Land?

5. What was the name of the volunteer group which encouraged women to help the war effort by working in agriculture?

6. Awarded for his actions at Mons on August 23 1914, who was the first private soldier to be awarded a Victoria Cross in the war?

7. What was an honour envelope?

8. In which small French village, liberated by the ANZACs, is there a sign in the village school, that was put up after the liberation and remains today, which reads ' Never Forget Australia'?

9. Which famous historian was appointed as Australia's Official War Correspondent in September 1914?

10. Who said after the Armistice: *The work is not over yet – the work of the nation, the work of the people, the work of those who have sacrificed. Let us work together first. What is our task? To make Britain a fit country for heroes to live in.*?

QUIZ 94 - THE GERMAN OFFENSIVE

Questions to tax your knowledge on Germany's big push to win the war in 1918:

1. The German Spring Offensive of 1918 is known by many names, the Ludendorff Offensive and the Kaiser's Battle being two, what impressive name did the German's give it?

2. Commencing on March 21 1918 what was the code name of the opening operation of the offensive which took place between Arras and St Quentin?

3. The British Third Army under the leadership of General Julian Byng was defending the area from Arras south to Flesquieres, which general was commanding the Fifth Army who were holding the longest front of the BEF?

4. Which General took over the command of Fifth Army on March 28 when the long retreat was deemed a failure of its commander?

5. Which German general was a great advocate but erroneously credited with creating the stormtrooper tactics that were so successful?

6. Also known as The Battle of the Lys, what was the second phase of the German offensive, launched on April 9 code named?

7. During the Battle of the Lys Private Anibal Milhais showed great courage in defending the retreating allied forces with just a machine gun. In the same offensive the Second Division of his army suffered catastrophic losses. For which army was Milhais fighting?

8. There were two other German offensives during the Spring Offensive, what were their codenames?

9. Commencing on July 15 and lasting until August 6 which battle was the last major offensive made by the Germans in the war which ultimately resulted in victory for the Allies and would create a springboard for winning the war?

10. Who was war correspondent, Floyd Gibbons referring to when he wrote *I never saw men charge to their death with finer spirit*?

QUIZ 95 - WHO WROTE THAT?

Identify the writer of these words:

1. In a letter to a friend in 1916 - *I think a curse should rest on me - because I love this war. I know it's smashing and shattering the lives of thousands every moment - and yet- I can't help it - I enjoy every second of it.*

2. A great American author of his own experiences - *World War One was the most colossal, murderous, mismanaged butchery that has ever taken place on earth. Any writer who said otherwise lied. So the writers either wrote propaganda, shut up, or fought.*

3. A British polymath - *We do not like to be robbed of an enemy; we want someone to have when we suffer. ... If so-and-so's wickedness is the sole cause of our misery, let us punish so-and-so and we shall be happy. The supreme example of this kind of political thought was the Treaty of Versailles. Yet most people are only seeking some new scapegoat to replace the Germans.*

4. A British officer and poet in a letter to his friend Marion Scott in February 1917 - *In the mind of all the English soldiers there is absolutely no hate for the Germans, but a kind of brotherly though slightly contemptuous kindness - as to men who are going through a bad time as well as ourselves.*

5. In his diary in October 1918 - *God would never be cruel enough to create a cyclone as terrible as that Argonne battle. Only man would ever think of doing an awful thing like that.*

6. French author and former soldier in his novel 'Le Feu' - *Two armies that fight each other is like one large army that commits suicide.*

7. An American statesman in 1924 in a letter to Charles Gardner - *During the war 500,000 coloured men and boys were called up under the draft, not one of whom sought to evade it. They took their places wherever assigned in defence of the nation of which they are just as truly citizens as are any others.*

8. A soldier of the Middle East campaign - *Yet when we achieved, and the new world dawned, the old men came out again and took our victory to remake it in the likeness of the former world they knew. Youth could win, but had not learned to keep: and was pitiably weak against age. We stammered that we had worked for a new heaven and a new earth, and they thanked us kindly and made their peace.*

9. Shortly before his death, a poet in a letter to a friend at Christmas 1914 - *It's all a terrible tragedy. And yet, in its details, it's great fun. And - apart from the tragedy - I've never felt happier or better in my life than in those days in Belgium.*

10. A German Admiral in a letter to his wife in October 1914 - *This war is really the greatest insanity in which white races have ever been engaged.*

QUIZ 96 - IN MEMORIAM 2

Some more questions to remind us how we remember those that were lost:

1. To whom is the memorial in the form of a flying stork on a roundabout in Poelkapelle, Belgium dedicated?

2. When was the Menin Gate Memorial unveiled?

3. An unusual cemetery in France, Cimetière Chinois de Nolette, is the burial place of 849 workers who died in the war, predominantly from an outbreak of cholera. What nationality were they?

4. There is an impressive memorial that stands under the southern edge of Mametz Wood to the 4000 men who became casualties between July 7-12 1916. From which country were they from?

5. What is the name of the huge obelisk monument in Turkey which commemorates the tens of thousands who were lost during the Gallipoli Campaign?

6. Who was the designer of the Tyne Cot Memorial and Cemetery?

7. There are four New Zealand Battlefield Memorials on the Western Front, where are they?

8. Opened in May 2001 where is the UK's National Memorial Arboretum?

9. What can be found at Vladslo and Langemarck in Belgium and Fricourt and Neuville-St-Vaast in France?

10. Who designed the extraordinary Canadian National Memorial on Vimy Ridge in France?

QUIZ 97 - VISITING THE WAR SITES TODAY 2

A second selection of questions on what can be visited today for those with an interest in the First World War:

1. Next to the village of Longueval in the Somme region, which infamous wood today houses the South African National Memorial and Museum?

2. What did the Newfoundlanders nickname the marker from the Somme Offensive still found in Newfoundland Memorial Park, about halfway through No Man's Land?

3. What is the name of the graceful circular structure which is flanked by two lions, adjacent to the Berkshire Cemetery where you can hear the playing of the Last Post at 7 p.m. on the first Friday of every month?

4. In which Belgian village is the Memorial Museum Passchendaele 1917?

5. The impressively titled World Centre For Peace, Liberties and Human Rights is a must-visit in Verdun. In what equally as impressive building does it reside?

6. What extraordinary red stone monolith, standing 33 metres high which contains in bas relief a host of Allied commanders can be found at Mondemont in France?

7. What is the 'name' of the outstanding example of an original battlefield tank that now resides in a small museum in Flesquieres?

8. Where are the preserved Belgian trenches where a memorial states *Here our Army held the invader in check 1914 – 1918*?

9. Funded variously by the Touring Club de France, Touring Club de Belgique and the Ypres League, what is the name of the one metre high monuments found along the Western Front which denote the points at which the Allies launched their offensive against the Germans in the summer of 1918?

10. What is the name of the excellent, modern museum that has been opened close to Pheasant Wood Cemetery, completed in July 2010, the first new war cemetery built by the Commonwealth War Graves Commission in fifty years?

QUIZ 98 - LAST HUNDRED DAYS

Ten questions on the last days of the war:

1. Also known as the Third Battle of Picardy, this successful attack on August 8 1918 saw the commencement of the Hundred Days Offensive and was in large part the brainchild of the brilliant Australian commander Lt Gen John Monash. What was the name of the battle?

2. Killed by a sniper on August 18 1918, what was the name of Military Medal and bar holder that was an indigenous Canadian and himself an elite sniper?

3. The location of the deepest penetration of Allied Forces on the first day of the above battle, where is the official memorial commemorating the Canadian victory situated?

4. Having been awarded a Military Cross in September 1918, who was awarded a Victoria Cross for his actions at Pont-sur-Sambre on November 6 1918, the final Victoria Cross awarded actions of the war?

5. Beginning on September 29 1918, victory in which battle saw the first full breach of the Germans' resistance on the Hindenberg Line?

6. General Henry Rawlinson commanded the British Fourth Army in the breach of the Hindenberg Line. As well as British troops, what two other countries were significantly represented in that army?

7. The last Canadian soldier to be killed on the Western Front was Private George Price at 10.58 a.m. on November 11 1918, the victim of a sniper's bullet. In which cemetery is he buried?

8. Although named the Last Hundred Days Offensive, how many days were there actually between the commencement on August 8 and the end on November 11 1918?

9. Which offensive commencing on September 6 and lasting until the Armistice was the principal offensive of the American Expeditionary Force in which 1.2 million soldiers of which 26,277 were killed?

10. Reaching Mons at 4 a.m. on November 11, which were the liberating troops of this Belgian town?

QUIZ 99 - THANK GOD IT'S ALL OVER!

For the penultimate round of questions, a look at the immediate aftermath of the war:

1. Which of the Central Powers was the first to surrender?

2. After Wilhelm II was ousted from power, who took control and led the peace negotiations for Germany?

3. On what date did British and American forces enter Germany?

4. The armistice was first negotiated in a train car, where was it stationed?

5. Upon what date was the Treaty of Versailles signed?

6. Who were the 'Big Four' at the Paris Peace Conference?

7. What was the name of the international organisation created after the First World War with the intention to ensure peace?

8. On which date did the Treaty of Versailles begin to take effect?

9. In what year was the Geneva Convention signed which, amongst other things, restricted the use of chemical and biological agents in warfare?

10. What was the cut-off date for the provision of an Imperial War Graves headstone for those dying from the effects of the conflict?

QUIZ 100 - THE FINAL WORD

Finally, questions which are perhaps speculative and the answers open to conjecture. This round is about reflection on the cost of the Great War.

1. How long was the war?

2. To the nearest million, globally, what is the best estimate of how many people fought in the war?

3. To the nearest half million, how many troops are thought to have been killed in total in the war?

4. Of the Allied Powers, who suffered the highest number of military deaths?

5. Of the Central Powers who suffered the highest number of military deaths?

6. To the nearest ten thousand, how many British Empire servicemen were killed in the war?

7. How many countries fought in the war?

8. How many civilians globally, to the nearest million, are thought to have been killed during the war?

9. How many horses and mules, to the nearest ten thousand, died on the Western Front?

10. How many Armenians are estimated to have been murdered in the mass genocide by the Ottoman Empire?

11. What was the estimated contemporary financial cost of the war?

12. How many people are estimated to have died in the Spanish flu pandemic of 1918-19?

Added to these figures should be considered the catastrophic number of wounded and displaced, and the malnutrition and disease caused by wartime shortages which directly affected not only the generation that lived through the war but also those that followed.

THE ANSWERS

QUIZ 1 - NICE AND EASY DOES IT

1. France, Russia and Great Britain
2. August 4th 1914
3. No Man's Land
4. Germany, Austria-Hungary, Italy
5. Lice
6. The Red Baron
7. They were the flares fired by Very pistols usually at night to illuminate No-Man's Land
8. Pill box
9. The Victoria Cross
10. 11 a.m. November 11 1918

QUIZ 2 - WINDS OF WAR

1. 1839
2. Alsace-Lorraine
3. Robert Gascoyne-Cecil (then Prime Minister of Great Britain)
4. 1907
5. Agadir Crisis
6. Jean Jaures
7. Sarajevo
8. Austria-Hungary
9. Tsar Nicholas II of Russia
10. Herbert Asquith (British Prime Minister)

QUIZ 3 - IT STARTS

1. Gavril Princip
2. The Black Hand
3. Austria-Hungary
4. July 28 1914
5. The Skirmish of Joncherey
6. Liege
7. 735,000
8. Edward Grey
9. Mons
10. Field Marshal Sir John French

QUIZ 4 - GENERAL KNOWLEDGE 1

1. Sophie
2. Rupprecht, Crown Prince of Bavaria and Kaiser Wilhelm II
3. Cobbers
4. 5' 3" (this was later reduced)
5. Geoffrey Malins and John McDowell
6. Switzerland (at Pfetterhouse)
7. Fire the first British shot of the war
8. Vera Brittain
9. Pip, Squeak and Wilfred (from the Daily Mirror comic strip - Pip was a dog,

Squeak and penguin and Wilfred a baby rabbit)
10. Hindustani, meaning dust coloured.

QUIZ 5 - MILITARY BREAKDOWN

1. Commanded no-one!
2. A section or 12 men
3. A platoon of 50 men
4. A company of 200 men
5. A battalion of 1000 men
6. A brigade of 3,500 men
7. A division of 12,000 men
8. A corps of 60,000 men
9. An army of 300,000 men
10. An army group of 2,000,000 men

QUIZ 6 - INITIALLY SPEAKING

1. British Expeditionary Force
2. Royal Flying Corps
3. District Court Martial
4. Voluntary Aid Detachment
5. Princess Patricia's Canadian Light Infantry
6. Distinguished Service Order
7. Australian Imperial Force
8. Casualty Clearing Station
9. Short Magazine Lee Enfield
10. Women's Army Auxiliary Corps

QUIZ 7 - RANK AND FILE

1. Admiral of the Fleet
2. Aspirant
3. Lieutenant Colonel
4. The Ottoman Empire Army
5. Three
6. Lieutenant Colonel (and similarly for British and U.S. etc)
7. Capitano
8. Major-General, Brigadier-General, Colonel, Lieutenant-Colonel, Major, Captain.
9. Coronel
10. Generalfeldmarschall

QUIZ 8 - NAME THE COUNTRY

1. Turkey
2. Italy
3. Poland
4. Bulgaria
5. Serbia
6. Tanzania
7. Greece

8. Egypt
9. Iraq
10. France

QUIZ 9 - TOMMYS' SLANG 1
1. Run away or clear out (from the French *allez tout de suite*)
2. Socks
3. Cook
4. Meat pudding
5. To go mad or lose your nerve
6. A big man (regular army term from India)
7. Duckboards
8. Steel helmet
9. Money
10. England or home

QUIZ 10 - WORLD LEADERS 1
1. Herbert Asquith
2. Woodrow Wilson
3. Vasil Radoslavov
4. Nicholas II
5. Victor Emmanuel III
6. Mehmed V
7. Albert I
8. Wilhelm II
9. Alfonso XIII
10. Taisho (Yoshihito)

QUIZ 11 - ANAGRAMS 1
1. Field Marshal Douglas Haig
2. Edith Cavell
3. Wilfred Owen
4. Valentine Joe Strudwick
5. Baron von Richthofen
6. Nellie Spindler
7. Fabian Ware
8. Marshal Ferdinand Foch
9. William Leefe Robinson
10. Archduke Franz Ferdinand

QUIZ 12 - GENERAL KNOWLEDGE 2
1. Poperinge
2. Vancouver Corner, St Juliaan, Ypres
3. A salient is when your lines jut so far into the enemy's that you can be fired upon by multiple sides.
4. Japan
5. They were shot at dawn

6. Captain Fred Roberts
7. The Gallipoli Peninsula
8. Pickelhaube
9. Newfoundland
10. Lieutenant Henry Webber, aged 67, killed at Mametz Wood on the Somme July 21 1916

QUIZ 13 - ARMY SIGNALLER'S CODE 1

1. Monkey
2. Don
3. London
4. William
5. Nuts
6. Toc
7. Queen
8. Sugar
9. Ack
10. Johnnie

QUIZ 14 - WHO AM I? 1

1. Roland Garros
2. C.S. Lewis
3. Gerard Leman
4. Billy Butlin
5. A.A.Milne
6. Raymond Asquith
7. Henry Williamson
8. J.R.R.Tolkien
9. R.C. Sherriff
10. Guillauume Apollinaire

QUIZ 15 - IT'S A DATE 1

1. June 28 1914
2. August 3 1914
3. August 22 1914
4. May 23 1915
5. May 24 1915
6. December 20 1915
7. March 2 1916
8. July 1 1916 (first day of the Battle of the Somme)
9. June 17 1917
10. November 11 1918 at 9.30 a.m., at Mons, just 90 minutes before the ceasefire - the last British soldier to be killed in the war?

QUIZ 16 - POLITICIANS AT WAR

1. Arthur O'Neill
2. Anthony Eden

3. David Lindsay, 27th Earl of Crawford, 10th Earl of Balcarres
4. Harold Cawley
5. John Ward
6. Daniel Desmond Sheehan
7. First Lord of the Admiralty
8. Lord Ninian Crichton-Stuart
9. Sir Philip Sassoon
10. William Wedgwood Benn

QUIZ 17 - NAME THE BATTLE 1

1. The Battle of Messines
2. Battle of Jutland
3. Battle of Saint Mihiel
4. The Battle of the Marne
5. Battle of Verdun
6. Battle of the Somme
7. Battle of Chunuk Bair
8. Battle of Flers-Courcelette
9. Second Battle of Ypres
10. Battle of Aqaba

QUIZ 18 - THE CANADIANS

1. Halifax, Nova Scotia.
2. They landed at Suvla Bay on September 20 1915 and remained in the Gallipoli campaign until the final withdrawal of troops on January 9 1916
3. They took out their handkerchieves, urinated on them and put them over their mouths and noses.
4. Waterproof, leather knee-boots
5. Lieutenant Colonel William Barker
6. July 1 (because of the devastation to the Newfoundlanders on the first day of the Battle of the Somme)
7. The Battle of Vimy Ridge April 9 - 12 1917
8. November 6 1917
9. Major George Pearkes
10. The Battle of Canal du Nord as they fought to capture Bourlon Wood in September 1918

QUIZ 19 - ALL AT SEA 1

1. H.M.S. Dreadnought
2. H.M.S. Amphion
3. The Battle of Heligoland Bight
4. Prince Louis Alexander of Battenberg (as public opinion was against a German prince being in charge of the British navy!)
5. Maximilian von Spee
6. S.M.S. Emden
7. Contact mines
8. H.M.S. Hampshire

9. The Zeebrugge Raid
10. Tirpitz, a pig

QUIZ 20 - ANAGRAMS 2

1. Hindenburg Line
2. Tyne Cot Cemetery
3. Beaumont Hamel
4. Spanbroekmolen mine crater
5. Pozieres
6. Fromelles
7. Vancouver Corner
8. Gallipoli
9. Versailles
10. Caporetto

QUIZ 21 - MEDICAL ADVANCEMENTS

1. The Thomas Splint
2. Plastic surgery, in particular facial reconstruction
3. Gas Gangrene
4. Alexander Fleming
5. Artificial limbs, particularly legs. This included helping the standardisation of false limbs and increasingly using light metals in their manufacture.
6. George Crile
7. Harvey Cushing
8. The Carrel-Dakin Technique, after British biochemist Henry Dakin who discovered the solution and French doctor Alexis Carrel who utilised it but insisted on the opening of wounds to fully cleanse.
9. Marie Curie (the ambulances were quickly nicknamed 'Petites Curies')
10. Sodium Citrate – an anticoagulant (first used by Belgian doctor Albert Hustin in 1914)

QUIZ 22 - GENERAL KNOWLEDGE 3

Bruce Bairnsfather
1st Battalion Grenadier Guards
The Post Office
Vesta Tilley
The Military Police
John Condon, Royal Irish Regiment, 14 years of age.
In Flanders Fields
Portland Stone
Maconochie
Whilst undercovers they resembled water tanks or, another belief is that to keep them secret, workers creating the new weapon were told that they were going to be used to take water to the front lines.

QUIZ 23 - IT'S ALL ABOUT THE NUMBERS 1

1. 11
2. 179
3. 0
4. 60
5. 19
6. 141 (July 1 - November 18 1916)
7. 35,000
8. 78
9. 12 (Sidney Lewis who enlisted in the East Surrey Regiment in 1915 and saw action on the Somme)
10. 73

QUIZ 24 - THE WAR ON THE HOME FRONT

1. The Defence of the Realm Act of 1914 empowering the government to do almost anything necessary to help the war effort and protect the country.
2. Scarborough, Hartlepool and Whitby
3. Great Yarmouth and Kings Lynn
4. White feathers
5. Britain suffered its worst railway disaster when 226 people were killed (2214 of them soldiers) when a troop train crashed into a stationary train, and was then itself struck by the Glasgow Express.
6. Daylight Saving Time (first used in Germany in April 1916, Britain first advanced clocks an hour from May 21 1916 to October 1)
7. The Times
8. The conkers were used to produce acetone which would then be used in the production of cordite to be used in bullets and shells.
9. Eight tons of TNT exploded at a munitions factory causing the deaths of 134 people of which only 32 could be identified
10. 1918 (sugar, meat, flour, milk and butter)

QUIZ 25 - ITALY

1. Antonio Salandra
2. Treaty of London (or Pact of London) which would effectively bring Italy into the war on the side of the Triple Entente
3.Luigi Cadorna
4. Riccardo Giusto
5. He only had one leg – having lost the other in an accident in 1908.
6. The White War
7. Battle of Vittorio Veneto
8. November 3 1918
9. Allied Army of the Orient
10. Regia Marina (simply – Royal Navy)

QUIZ 26 - IT'S AN ANIMAL THING

1. Caribou (the mascot of the Newfoundlanders)
2. Horse (Warrior was Captain Seeley's famous horse, posthumously awarded a

Dickin Medal in 2014)
3. Kangaroo (the mascot)
4. Rats
5. Cat (Togo was the mascot of the famous ship)
6. Pigeon (a messenger pigeon used by the U.S. Army Signal Corps that was awarded the Croix de Guerre for her delivery of a message during the Meuse-Argonne Offensive that saved the lives of many soldiers)
7. Donkey (Australian stretcher-bearer Kirkpatrick famously used donkeys to bring first aid and ferry wounded soldiers back to the beaches)
8. Bear (Canadian veterinarian Colebourn rescued the orphan black bear and brought her with him on his way to the Western Front, but left her for safe keeping at London Zoo where she became famous and an inspiration to A.A.Milne)
9. Elephant (Lizzie the elephant was leased by scrap metal dealer Ward to help transport machinery around Sheffield, England after his horses had been requisitioned for war service)
10. Baboon (Jackie was the Infantry's mascot who saw action with them on the Western Front where he was wounded and had to have a leg amputated. Happily he did return to South Africa after the War)

QUIZ 27 - GALLIPOLI

1. Admiral Carden, however three days before the main attack he fell seriously ill and had to resign.
2. The French battleship Bouvet which struck a mine on March 18 1915 and sunk within 2 minutes
3. S, V, W, X and Y. Y, V and W saw the worst casualties.
4. Baby 700
5. Admiral John Fisher
6. Dysentery
7. Mustafa Kemal Ataturk
8. It was torpedoed by the German Submarine U21
9. William Birdwood
10. It is the only marked Allied grave not found in a cemetery.

QUIZ 28 - IT'S ALL UP IN THE AIR 1

1. In order to stop their own troops from shooting them down.
2. They were named after their builder Count Ferdinand von Zeppelin
3. William Avery Bishop
4. Fokker Eindecker
5. Italy
6. Lieutenant Albert Ball
7. A long range bomber
8. April 1 1918
9. The Sopwith Salamander
10. Fritz Anders

QUIZ 29 - STARS IN THE WARS

1. Basil Rathbone
2. Arnold Ridley
3. Maurice Chevalier
4. Ronald Colman.
5. Fritz Lang
6. Bela Lugosi
7. Claude Rains
8. Nigel Bruce
9. Randolph Scott
10. Humphrey Bogart

QUIZ 30 - WHAT'S THE REAL NAME? 1

1. Ypres
2. Mouquet Farm
3. Albert
4. Sailly la Bourse
5. Bailleul
6. Poperinghe
7. Wytschaete
8. Hebuterne
9. Ploegsteert Wood
10. Delville Wood

QUIZ 31 - NAME THE POEM AND ITS AUTHOR

1. *The Soldier*, Rupert Brooke
2. *The Hero*, Siegfried Sassoon
3. *In a Cafe,* Francis Ledwidge
4. *To Germany*, Charles Sorley
5. *Dulce et Decorum Est,* Wilfred Owen
6. *The Dead Fox Hunter*, Robert Graves
7. *Louse Hunting,* Isaac Rosenberg
8. *The Silent One*, Ivor Gurney
9. *Rain*, Philip Thomas
10. *The Zonnebeke Road*, Edmund Blunden

QUIZ 32 - ANAGRAMS 3

1. Mustard Gas
2. Vickers Machine Gun
3. Maxim Gun
4.Zeppelin
5. Stokes Mortar
6. Big Bertha
7. Mills Bomb
8. Flammenwerfer
9. Lee Enfield
10. Dreadnought

QUIZ 33 - GENERAL KNOWLEDGE 4

1. Bantam Battalions
2. Dough Boys
3. Dominion of Newfoundland and India.
4. The opening of the canal locks of the Ieperlee Canal and Yser River which flooded the low ground.
5. The first 100,000 of Lord Kitchener's New Army volunteers
6. Romanov
7. The Battle of Loos
8. Francis Ledwidge
9. Gelibolu
10. John Norton-Griffiths (known as Empire Jack and grandfather of Jeremy Thorpe)

QUIZ 34 - NAME THE VICTORIA CROSS WINNER

1. William Leefe Robinson
2. William (Billy) McFadzean
3. Naik Shahamad Khan
4. Lieutenant Arthur Martin-Leake
5. Mir Dast
6. Lieutenant William Sanders
7. Private John Caffrey
8. Private Albert Halton
9. Captain William Bishop
10. Lance Corporal William Coltman

QUIZ 35 - RUSSIA

1. July 28 1914, after Austria-Hungary declared war on Serbia, Russia's ally
2. Sergei Sazonov
3. Alexander Samsonov
4. The first air-to-air kill (by ramming an Austrian aeroplane)
5. The Ottoman Empire
6. Xylyl Bromide
7. The Brusilov Offensive
8. Rennenkampf
9. Alexander Kerensky
10. A declaration of peace

QUIZ 36 - NAME THAT TUNE

1. Mademoiselles from Armentieres
2. It's A Long Way To Tipperary
3. Pack Up Your Troubles
4. When This Lousy War Is Over
5. Keep The Homes Fires Burning
6. If You Were The Only Girl In The World.
7. I Wore A Tunic

8. Goodbye-ee
9. Roses of Picardy
10. Over There

QUIZ 37 - THE HISTORIANS 1
1. Martin Middlebrook
2. Alan Clark
3. Robert Graves
4. George Coppard
5. Peter Simkins
6. Lyn MacDonald
7. B.H. Liddell Hart
8. Ernst Junger
9. T.E. Lawrence
10. Alistair Horne

QUIZ 38 - WHERE AM I BURIED?
1. St Symphorien Military Cemetery, Hainaut, Belgium.
2. Farm Cemetery, West-Vlaanderen, Belgium
3. Sanctuary Wood Cemetery, Ypres, Belgium
4. St Mary's A.D.S. Cemetery, Haisnes, Pas De Calais, France
5. Ors Communal Cemetery, Nord, France
6. No known grave, commemorated on the Thiepval Memorial, Somme, France
7. Brandhoek New Military Cemetery, Ypres
8. Skyros, Greece
9. Norwich Cathedral
10. No known grave, commemorated on the Hollybrook Memorial, Southampton

QUIZ 39 - CAPITAL CITIES
1. Kristiania
2. Vienna
3. Munich
4. Dresden
5. Stuttgart
6. Saint Petersburg
7. Durres
8. Constantinople
9. Rio de Janeiro
10. St John's

QUIZ 40 - INSPECTING THE MORSE
1. M
2. O
3. R
4. S
5. E
6. C

7. D
8. W
9. 1
10. 4

QUIZ 41 - I SPY

1. Carl Lody (November 6 1914)
2. Twelve
3. He was hanged at Wandsworth Jail whilst all the others were shot by a firing squad at dawn at the Tower of London
4. William Somerset Maugham
5. Mata Hari
6. Edith Cavell
7. Arthur Ransome
8.Elsbeth Schragmuller
9. Gabrielle Petit (there is a statue of her in Place Saint-Jean, Brussels)
10. Deuxieme Bureau

QUIZ 42 - ANAGRAMS 4

1. In Flanders Fields
2. Leaning Virgin of Albert
3. Victoria Cross
4. Pack Up Your Troubles
5. Schlieffen Plan
6. Fraternisation with the enemy
7. Mademoiselle from Armentiere
8. Pip, Squeak and Wilfred
9. Angels of Mons
10. British Expeditionary Force

QUIZ 43 - GENERAL KNOWLEDGE 5

1. Livens Projector
2. Both were licensed brothels, but the blue lamps were for the benefit of officers.
3. The British War Medal and the Victory Medal of 1919 (taken from popular comic paper characters of the time)
4. Parados
5. King George V (Great Britain), Kaiser Wilhelm II (Germany), Tsar Nicholas II (Russia)
6. The creeping barrage
7. Battle of the Yser (Oct 16 – 31 1914)
8. Ploegsteert (Plugstreet to the Tommies)
9. The cyclist battalions
10. A big Turkish gun situated at the Dardanelles

QUIZ 44 - BELGIUM

1. Liechtenstein
2. Diksmuide

3. To terrify the Belgian citizens into not rebelling. This would often include executions for those that would not line up alongside the roadsides to watch the German soldiers marching past.
4. The Rape of Belgium
5. Charles de Broqueville
6. Le Havre in France
7. General Moritz von Bissing (died in Brussels, Belgium April 18 1917)
8. The wire of death – a lethal electric fence that claimed the lives of 2-3000 Belgian refugees
9. Belgian Expeditionary Corps of Armoured Cars (ACM) – 400 soldiers and 10 armoured cars
10. The state paid returning Belgians 3000 Belgian Francs to purchase materials to build their own homes. Therefore these homes became known as the 3000s – Drieduusters

QUIZ 45 - GERMANY
1. General Alexander von Kluck, the commander of the German First Army in 1914
2. The Emden
3. Shutte-Lanz
4. Maximilian von Spee
5. Oswald Boelcke
6. German Chief of General Staff, General Erich von Falkenhayn
7. Adolf Hitler
8. Operation Alberich
9. Tanks
10. Erich Ludendorff

QUIZ 46 - NAME THE FILM
1. Legends of the Fall
2. Paths of Glory
3. Tolkien
4. The Blue Max
5. Darling Lili
6. Ryan's Daughter
7. The Trench
8. Gallipoli
9. 1917
10. Wonder Woman

QUIZ 47 - TOMMYS' SLANG 2
1. Sniper (from some snipers noting their successes by carving notches in the butts of their guns)
2. No worries, it doesn't matter (from the French ca ne fait rien)
3. The infantry (due to their heavy packs)
4. A Highland soldier
5. Louse (a familiar enemy of the men in the trenches)

6. Food (from the French verb *manger* to eat)
7. Arrested
8. Machine Gun (M.G.)
9. Very Lights
10. Bully beef and biscuits eaten cold and uncooked.

QUIZ 48 – THE BATTLE OF THE SOMME

1. Picardy
2. Albert and Bapaume
3. It was the only occasion that cavalry would be used during the Somme campaign
4. French Foreign Legion
5. Mash Valley
6. Schwaben Redoubt
7. Noel Chavasse
8. Harold Macmillan
9. The tank
10. Because the killed and wounded from earlier attacks blocked the front trenches.

QUIZ 49 - WOMEN AT WAR

1. The marriage bar required that the majority of female employees had to resign from their jobs when they got married.
2. 1,600,000
3. Grace D Bunker
4. Dorothy Lawrence
5. Nellie Spindler
6. Ettie Rout
7. Eliane Cossey
8. The Women's Battalion of Death
9. Royal Serbian Army (She became a sergeant major during the war and was promoted to captain afterwards)
10. Those over 30 years of age.

QUIZ 50 - IT'S A DATE 2

1. August 8 1914
2. May 7 1915
3. May 31 1915
4. February 21 1916
5. May 16 1916
6. February 3 1917
7. March 1 1917
8. December 15 1917
9. March 21 1918
10. May 28 1918

QUIZ 51 - TAKE IT EASY

1. Westminster Abbey
2. Indiana Jones

3. The Spanish Flu pandemic
4. Stand To
5. Vladimir Lenin
6. Australian and New Zealand Army Corps
7. Schlieffen Plan
8. George VI
9. July 1 1916
10. The Treaty of Versailles

QUIZ 52 - FOR THE EXPERTS ONLY!

1. East Galicia
2. October 26 1917
3. Algerian soldiers serving in the light infantry of the French army.
4. Kaiserliche Marine
5. Rudyard Kipling
6. Japan
7. Sergeant Hugh Cairns of the 46th Battalion, who then died of his wounds on November 2 1918.
8. The Battle of Mont Saint-Quentin (August 31 – September 4 1918)
9. August 25 1914 they were being used for patrol purposes over the retreating British forces in France.
10. Italian air power theorist Giulio Douhet who appreciated the advantages of air power, and said that it should be a separate entity to the conventional army.

QUIZ 53 - ARMY SIGNALLER'S CODE 2

1. Yellow
2. Beer
3. King
4. Pip
5. Vic
6. Edward
7. Harry
8. Zebra
9. Ink
10. Uncle

QUIZ 54 - GENERAL KNOWLEDGE 6

1. A brand of brass polish popular amongst the troops to clean badges and buttons.
2. Phosgene
3. Queen Elisabeth
4. Trench Mortar Bombs
5. Per Adua Ad Astra (Through Adversity to the Stars)
6. Rosemary, which is found growing wild on the Gallipoli Peninsula
7. Harry Patch
8. Poperinghe
9. S.R.D. (for Service Rum Diluted)
10. Puttee

QUIZ 55 - INVENTORS AND INVENTIONS

1. Dutch
2. A steel helmet (Brodie's Steel Helmet)
3. Kotex sanitary pads
4. Stainless Steel
5. Pilates (the bodybuilder was Joseph Hubertus Pilates)
6. Watches
7. Captain Oswald Robertson
8. Zippers
9. Kleenex tissues for men (as an alternative to handkerchieves)
10. A vegetarian sausage containing soy. He developed it to counteract the food shortages in his home town of Cologne

QUIZ 56 - THE NEW ZEALANDERS

1. Kiwis
2. The seizure of German Samoa on August 29 1914
3. Egypt
4. Lieutenant Colonel William Malone
5. Caterpillar Valley Cemetery, Longueval, Somme
6. The Unlucky Otagos
7. 11 (though several were earned by New Zealanders attached to other countries)
8. It is the first and only such medal to be awarded to a New Zealander serving with a naval force.
9. The New Zealand Division disbanded on March 25 1919
10. 42%

QUIZ 57 - THE HOME FRONT

1. Charlie Chaplin
2. Steve Donoghue
3. Sheffield United
4. Sir Harry Lauder
5. Jess Willard
6. Saxe-Coburg and Gotha
7. H.G. Wells
8. W.C. Handy
9. 1916
10. Fairies (the Cottingley Fairies)

QUIZ 58 - IT'S A GENERAL THING

1. John Monash
2. Sir David Henderson
3. Paul von Arras
4. General Aylmer Hunter-Weston
5. Lieutenant General Bernard Freyberg
6. Otto Liman von Sanders
7. Edmund Allenby

8. Lieutenant General Arthur Currie
9. Grand Duke Nicholas Nikolaevich
10. Field Marshal Herbert Plumer

QUIZ 59 - INITIALLY SPEAKING 2

1. Canadian Expeditionary Force
2. Distinguished Flying Cross
3. Army Ordnance Corps
4. Quartermaster General
5. General Officer Commanding
6. Heavy Branch Machine Gun Corps
7. Royal Naval Division
8. Army Cyclist Corps
9. British War Medal
10. American Expeditionary Force

QUIZ 60 - CURRENCY AFFAIRS

1. Canadian dollar
2. French Franc
3. Krone (or Korona)
4. Russian Ruble
5. Japanese Yen
6. Papiermark
7. Ottoman Lira
8. Australian Pound
9. Rupee
10. German East African Rupie

QUIZ 61 - WHO SAID THAT?

1. Kaiser Wilhelm II
2. Andrew Fisher
3. Field Marshal and Commander-in-Chief Joseph Joffre
4. David Lloyd George
5. Harold Harmsworth (Lord Rothermere)
6. Foch
7. David Lloyd George
8. Edward Grey (then Foreign Secretary)
9. H.G. Wells
10. George Santayana

QUIZ 62 - ANAGRAMS 6

1. Thiepval Memorial
2. Langemark
3. Loos En Gohelle
4. Douaumont Ossuary
5. Vimy Ridge
6. Lochnagar Crater

7. Mametz Wood
8. Messines Ridge
9. Hohenzollern Redoubt
10. Dardanelles

QUIZ 63 - GENERAL KNOWLEDGE 7

1. The First Battle of Ypres
2. Britons Lord Kitchener (in the form of a portrait of the man pointing) Wants You (also 'Your Country Needs You')
3. 'Male' tanks had two six pounder guns and four machine guns,' female' tanks had six machine guns.
4. Tickler's
5. Alvin Cullum York (Sergeant York)
6. Wilfred Owen
7. Sepoy
8. Woodbine Willie (a poet and priest renowned for giving out Woodbine cigarettes along with solace and comfort during the war to wounded and dying men)
9. Henry Thridgould (who had emigrated to New York in 1911 but returned to serve in the war)
10. War crinoline

QUIZ 64 - IT'S ALL ABOUT THE NUMBERS 2

1. 628
2. Only 68
3. 103 (July 31 - November 10)
4. 51
5. 20
6. 14
7. 18
8. 19
9. 99
10. 64

QUIZ 65 - INDIA

1. September 30 1914
2. General James Willcocks
3. Khudadad Khan
4. Seven (labelled A-G, i.e. IEFA, IEFB, IEFC etc)
5. Captain
6. 11
7. Mohandas Karamchand Gandhi (Mahatma Gandhi)
8. 1,440,437 (of which 877, 068 were combatants, 563,369 non-combatants)
9. Battle of Loos (September 1915)
10. It's the Neuve-Chappelle Indian Memorial on the Richebourg Road

QUIZ 66 - BATTLE OF ARRAS

1. April 9 1917
2. The Nivelle Offensive
3. Harry Cator
4. Vimy Ridge (April 9 – 12)
5. General Edmund Allenby
6. Scotsman Alexander 'Sandy' Turnbull who served in the Middlesex and East Surrey Regiments attaining the rank of lance-sergeant.
7. General Hugh Trenchard
8. Ludwig von Falkenhausen
9. Bullecourt
10. May 16 1917

QUIZ 67 - WORLD LEADERS 2

1. Sir Robert Borden
2. Raymond Poincare
3. Manuel Jose de Arriaga
4. William Massey
5. Louis Botha
6. Ion C. Bratianu
7. Nikola Pasic
8. Paul Eyschen
9. Franz Joseph
10. Constantine I

QUIZ 68 - WHAT'S THE REAL NAME 2?

1. Vlamertinghe
2. Rue du Bois (near Neuve Chapelle)
3. Doingt (near Peronne)
4. Fonquevillers
5. Hazebrouck
6. Hopoutre (a suburb of Poperinghe)
7. Gallipoli
8. Rouen
9. Leuze Wood
10. Auchonvillers

QUIZ 69 - A QUESTION OF SPORT

1. Rugby League, playing right wing for Hull FC
2. Rugby Union, Harlequins, Liverpool and England, he won 17 England caps and captained them for their four games in 1914.
3. Australian Rules Football
4. World Number 1 Tennis Player (11 Grand Slam titles, 6 in singles, 5 in doubles – including Wimbledon four times)
5. Rugby Union, Gloucester and England (four caps)
6. The first professional footballer to enlist in the British Army.
7. Ice Hockey – Ottawa Hockey Club 1903 - 1906

8. Rowing
9. Rugby Union, Northampton and England (7 caps)
10. Cricket, Kent and England (19 caps). Regarded as one of the best bowlers in history, with over 2500 first class wickets.

QUIZ 70 - NAME THE AUTHOR

1. Erich Maria Remarque
2. Sebastian Faulks
3. Michael Morpurgo
4. Ernest Hemingway
5. Rebecca West
6. Ford Madox Ford
7. Pat Barker
8. W.E. Johns
9. Sebastian Barry
10. Jaroslav Hasek

QUIZ 71 – THE GREAT WAR IN AFRICA

1. Schutztruppe
2. Lake Tanganyika
3. Lieutenant George Masterman Thompson
4. Battle of Sandfontein
5. Jan Smuts
6. Portugal
7. Major Carl Heinrich Zimmermann
8. Morocco
9. Chilembwe Uprising
10. General Paul von Lettow-Vorbeck (leading a guerilla campaign against the British in East Africa he didn't hear about the surrender until November 14 1914)

QUIZ 72 - ANAGRAMS 7

1. Kaiser Bill
2. Georges Clemenceau
3. Rudyard Kipling
4. Noel Godfrey Chavasse
5. Woodbine Willie
6. John Pershing
7. Billy McFadzean
8. Lord Kitchener
9. Erich Maria Remarque
10. Gavrilo Princip

QUIZ 73 - GENERAL KNOWLEDGE 8

1. James Ramsay MacDonald
2. The ongoing regular 'harvesting' of shells, shrapnel, bullets and the ilk in the fields of Belgium and Northern France that contained the Western Front battlefields

3. Douglas Haig
4. Henry Rawlinson
5. Dr Noel Chavasse
6. Charles Fryatt
7. Because of the Easter Rising
8. Walking Wounded Collecting Station
9. Chlorine, Bromine, Mustard and Phosgene
10. A public statement announcing Britain's support for the establishment of a "national home for the Jewish people" in Palestine which was at that time part of the Ottoman Empire with a small Jewish population.

QUIZ 74 - VISITING THE WAR SITES TODAY 1

1. 8 p.m.
2. Arras
3. Peronne
4. The Pool of Peace
5. Fort Douamont
6. Newfoundland Park
7. Ypres
8. ANZAC Cove
9. The Chateau-Thierry American Monument
10. Auchonvillers, Somme, France.

QUIZ 75 - THE AUSTRALIANS

1. SS Pfalz
2. New South Wales
3. The Victorian Scottish
4. Emu
5. Joseph Cook
6. Attack on Fromelles (July 19-20 1916)
7. Pozieres
8. Albert Jacka
9. Diggers
10. Lieutenant Frank McNamara

QUIZ 76 - VIVE LA FRANCE

1. In a fleet of taxicabs
2. The Mill on the Meuse
3. Adolphe Célestin Pégoud
4. Ferdinand Foch
5. General Philippe Petain
6. Charles de Gaulle
7. Lebel Modèle 1886
8. A light infantry corps of the French army, originally Algerians.
9. 160,000 (162,440)
10. Rene Fonck

QUIZ 77 - ALL AT SEA 2

1. HMAS AE2
2. He scuttled it, as he didn't want it to be seized and shared amongst the Allies.
3. His Majesty's Hospital Ship
4. The Battle of the Dover Strait (in effect, the First Battle of the Dover Strait)
5. Hand to hand combat, as the Germans attempted to board the British ship *Broke*.
6. Prince Albert (who would become King George VI, he was on board HMS Collingwood)
7. Japan
8. The Siege of Tsingtao
9. Battle of the Strait of Otranto (a victory for Austria-Hungary over the combined navies of Great Britain, Italy and France.
10. Boy Seaman Jack Cornwell

QUIZ 78 - NAME THE BATTLE 2

1. Battle of Tannenburg
2. Battle of Dogger Bank
3. Battle of Neuve Chapelle
4. Battle of Transylvania
5. Battle of Pilckem Ridge
6. Battle of Caporetto
7. Battle of La Malmaison
8. Battle of El Buqqar Ridge
9. Second Battle of Villers-Bretonneux
10. Battle of Drocourt-Queant Line

QUIZ 79 - THIRD BATTLE OF YPRES

1. Belgium
2. July 31 1917
3. 3.50 a.m.
4. Field Marshall Douglas Haig
5. Gough Must Go
6. He wanted to bring in more artillery (Gough had favoured mass infantry attacks over a wide front, Plumer wanted to bombard the Germans then attack with the infantry over a narrow front)
7. Battle of Menin Road Ridge.
8. New Zealand
9. 27th (City of Winnipeg) Battalion
10. 860,000

QUIZ 80 - TOMMYS' SLANG 3

1. Makeshift grenades made from ...... jam tins!
2. Faint whilst on parade
3. Canadians (from Lord Byng being their commander)
4. A brothel
5. Trench periscope
6. Minenwerfer (German bomb thrower, or the bomb itself)

7. The Medical Officer
8. Civilian clothes
9. Finished, nothing or gone (from the French Il n'y en a plus - there is no more)
10. Portuguese

QUIZ 81 - MORE FILMS

1. Shoulder Arms (1918)
2. The Big Parade (1925)
3. Hells Angels
4. The Lost Patrol
5. The Road To Glory
6. La Grande Guerra
7. King and Country
8. Oh! What A Lovely War
9. Joyeux Noel
10. Passchendaele

QUIZ 82 - ANAGRAMS 8

1. Laurence Binyon
2. Woodrow Wilson
3. Geoffrey Malins
4. Erich Ludendorff
5. Bruce Bairnsfather
6. George Ellison
7. David Lloyd George
8. Joseph Joffre
9. Sir John French
10. Helmuth von Moltke

QUIZ 83 - GENERAL KNOWLEDGE 9

1. Romania
2. The 'Hello Girls'.
3. Princess Mary
4. The Blue Puttees
5. Trench fever was caused by men scratching the bites from body lice and by so doing rubbing the excreta from the insect into the wound causing them to get infected.
6. Siegfried Stellung
7. Siegfried Sassoon
8. The Armenians
9. Ivor Novello (music) & Lena Guilbert Ford (lyrics)
10. Indian Army

QUIZ 84 - IN MEMORIAM

1. Sir Fabian Ware
2. Tyne Cot Cemetery
3. Sir Reginald Blomfield

4. 40 or more
5. New Zealand and Newfoundland
6. Hall of Remembrance, Australian War Memorial, Canberra
7. 1932
8. 72,000 (72,337)
9. Sir Edwin Lutyens
10. Rudyard Kipling

QUIZ 85 - IT'S A DATE 3

1. November 5 1914
2. September 28 1915
3. October 6 1915
4. June 5 1916
5. December 18 1916
6. April 1 1917
7. May 25 1917
8. June 24 1917
9. November 2 1917
10. September 26 1918

QUIZ 86 - THE HISTORIANS 2

1. Edmund Blunden
2. Gary Sheffield
3. Frank Richards
4. Captain J C Dunn
5. Captain F C Hitchcock MC
6. Vera Brittain
7. William Orpen
8. John Keegan
9. Rose Coombs
10. Barbara Tuchman

QUIZ 87 - WHO AM I? 2

1. Winston Churchill
2. Bernard Montgomery
3. Tubby Clayton, (Rev Philip Clayton) custodian of Talbot House
4. Rudyard Kipling
5. Marshal Ferdinand Foch
6. Noel Coward
7. King George V
8. David Lloyd George
9. Hermann Goring
10. Rupert Brooke

QUIZ 88 - NAME THE COUNTRY 2

1. France
2. Belgium

3. Poland
4. Turkey
5. Italy
6. Belgium
7. Iraq
8. Azerbaijan
9. France
10. England

QUIZ 89 - IT'S ALL UP IN THE AIR 2

1. As reconnaissance of the enemy
2. 100 mph
3. Royal Flying Corps and Royal Naval Air Service
4. Five
5. With a black cross
6. Archie
7. Dogfights
8. Gothas
9. Balloon busting
10. Three, it was a triplane

QUIZ 90 – BEHIND ENEMY LINES

1. Patrick Fowler
2. Guise Chateau
3. Major Joseph Kane
4. Groningen, Holland
5. Gunther Pluschow
6. These were the German POW camps designated for the enlisted men
7. Brian Horrocks
8. Yozgad
9. Henri Giraud
10. Holzminden

QUIZ 91 - CHOOSE YOUR WEAPON

1. Chlorine.
2. Flammenwerfer (flamethrowers)
3. Little Willie
4. Bangalore Torpedo
5. A type of explosive, discovered at Lydd in Kent used in bombs and shells.
6. Renowned British heavy naval guns mounted on railway carriages near Arras in 1918
7. Mills Bombs
8. The Lewis Machine Gun
9. .303
10. Ross Rifle

QUIZ 92 - THE AMERICANS ARE COMING

1. April 6 1917
2. General John Pershing.
3. R.M.S. Lusitania
4. Mexico
5. Alan Seeger
6. The first U.S. civilian ship sunk by German U-boats
7. Frank Luke
8. Battle of Cantigny
9. The Battle of Belleau Wood
10. Henry Johnson

QUIZ 93 - GENERAL KNOWLEDGE 10

1. A foreign unit of volunteer Armenians, originally named *La Légion d'Orient* within the French Army which fought against the Ottoman Empire.
2. The Treaty of Sevres
3. Canaries
4. A periscope
5. The Women's Land Army
6. Private Sidney Godley
7. It was an envelope which allowed soldiers to write home with the knowledge that their letter wouldn't be opened and read by a superior officer.
8. Villers-Bretonneux, the village makes a point of commemorating ANZAC Day each year.
9. Charles Bean
10. David Lloyd George

QUIZ 94 - THE GERMAN OFFENSIVE

1. Kaiserschlacht
2. Operation Michael
3. General Hubert Gough
4. General Henry Rawlinson
5. General Oskar von Hutier
6. Operation Georgette
7. Portuguese
8. Gneisenau and Blucher-Yorck.
9. The Second Battle of the Marne
10. American troops

QUIZ 95 - WHO WROTE THAT?

1. Winston Churchill
2. Ernest Hemingway
3. Bertrand Russell
4. Ivor Gurney
5. Alvin (sergeant) York
6. Henri Barbusse
7. Calvin Coolidge

8. T.E.Lawrence
9. Rupert Brooke
10. Admiral von Tirpitz

QUIZ 96 - IN MEMORIAM 2
1. France's flying ace Georges Guynemer, their second highest scoring ace
2. June 24 1927
3. Chinese
4. Wales
5. Helles Memorial
6. Herbert Baker
7. s' Graventafel, Messines, Le Quesnoy and Longueval
8. Alrewas, Staffordshire
9. German Military Cemeteries
10. Walter Seymour Allward

QUIZ 97 - VISITING THE WAR SITES TODAY 2
1. Delville Wood
2. The Danger Tree. It would end up marking the spot where many of them fell on July 1 1916
3. The Ploegsteert Memorial To The Missing
4. Zonnebeke
5. The Archbishop's Palace
6. The National Monument to the Victories of the Marne
7. Deborah
8. Diksmuide
9. Demarcation Stones
10. The Museum of the Battle of Fromelles (Musee de la Bataille de Fromelles)

QUIZ 98 - LAST HUNDRED DAYS
1. Battle of Amiens
2. Henry Norwest
3. Le Quesnel, a little east of Amiens.
4. Lieutenant-Colonel Brett Mackay Cloutman
5. Battle of St Quentin Canal
6. Australian and American
7. St Symphorien Military Cemetery, Mons
8. 95
9. Meuse-Argonne Offensive
10. Canadian

QUIZ 99 - THANK GOD IT'S ALL OVER!
1. Bulgaria
2. Max von Baden
3. December 16 1918
4. near Compiegne, France
5. June 28 1919

6. Woodrow Wilson (U.S.A.), Georges Clemenceau (France), David Lloyd George (Great Britain), Vittorio Emanuele Orlando (Italy)
7. The League of Nations
8. January 10 1920
9. 1925
10. August 31 1921

QUIZ 100 - THE FINAL WORD

1. 4 years, 106 days (July 28 1914 – November 11 1918)
2. 65 million
3. 8.5 million (this is open to conjecture, some say 10 million is closer to reality)
4. Russia with an estimated 1,700,000
5. Germany with an estimated 1,773,700
6. 908,371
7. 32
8. 13 million (again this is open to conjecture, but regardless the scale was massive)
9. 256,000
10. 1.5 million, an act effectively camouflaged while the world was at war.
11. $208 billion ($147 billion for the Allies, $61 billion Central Powers)
12. Estimates vary from 20 – 50 million people died from the virus.

FURTHER READING

There are innumerable wonderful books detailing all aspects of the First World War. Here are just some of my favourites that I recommend thoroughly:

Beauty and the Sorrow (The) (2011) – Peter Englund
Before Endeavours Fade (1976) – Rose Coombs
Catastrophe (2014) – Max Hastings
First Day On The Somme (The) (1971) – Martin Middlebrook
Forgotten Voices of the First World War (2003) – Max Arthur
Goodbye To All That: An Autobiography (1929) – Robert Graves
Guns of August (The) (1962) – Barbara Tuchman
Kitchener's Army : The Raising of the New Armies, 1914-16 (1988) - Peter Simkins
Last Fighting Tommy (The) (2007) – Harry Patch with Richard van Emden
Major and Mrs Holt's Battlefield Guide to the Western Front – North (2007)
Major and Mrs Holt's Battlefield Guide to the Western Front – South (2012)
Old Soldiers Never Die (1933) – Frank Richards
Price of Glory: Verdun 1916 (The) (1962) – Alistair Horne
Storm of Steel (1920) – Ernst Junger
They Called It Passchendaele (1990) – Lyn MacDonald
Tommy: The British Soldier on the Western Front (2005) – Richard Holmes
Undertones of War (1928) – Edmund Blunden
With A Machine Gun To Cambrai (1968) – George Coppard

Printed in Poland
by Amazon Fulfillment
Poland Sp. z o.o., Wrocław